Warbirds 26th March, 1940. Gloster Gladiator probably on test from Gloucester flying over an anonymous Severn King at Beachley, Old Passage.

Courtesy Fox Photos

SEVERN ENTERPRISE
THE STORY OF THE OLD AND NEW
PASSAGE FERRIES

Christopher Jordan

ARTHUR H. STOCKWELL Ltd.,
Elms Court   Ilfracombe,
Devon

To my Mother and Father
who opened my eyes to
the world about me.

I am a pilgrim of the future
On the way forward from a journey
Made through the wisdom of the past.

Teilhard du Chardin

ISBN 0 7223 0967-8
Printed in Great Britain by
Arthur H. Stockwell Ltd
Elms Court Ilfracombe
Devon

ACKNOWLEDGEMENTS

This is the first full length book, to my knowledge, on an individual river crossing and therefore breaks new ground on what I feel has been hitherto a neglected branch of our recorded maritime and communication history.

During the preparation of my story I have been gratified by the scale of interest shown and thank all those who have put up with seemingly nonsensical questions and requests for material.

In particular I wish to thank Mr Enoch Williams and family for their advice, factual information and reminiscences supplied without which the latter portion of this book could not have been written. Former employees at Old Passage, Ron Blight, Percy Palmer, Ben Brown, Bill Groves; Horace Olney of the 1926 era and the late Geof. Groves were a fund of knowledge. John Alway of Aust and past librarians of the City of Bristol, who have accumulated a wealth of books and other records, I particularly thank for their historical material.

For illustrations I am indebted again to the Williams family and others acknowledged elsewhere who have permitted me to use their prints. To Barry Rogers my thanks for his patient preparation of photographs suitable for inclusion.

As far as possible I have tried to verify all the many statements of fact, for the errors I apologize in advance. I have included all the material known to me at this time of writing but would be pleased to hear of anything further. Inevitably the tale roams from the historical through anecdote to technical for the sake of completeness. I ask your indulgence. Finally my thanks to my wife for her interest and support, not least on the typewriter.

April 1976

Christopher Jordan,
Spindrift,
17 Russet Close,
Olveston.

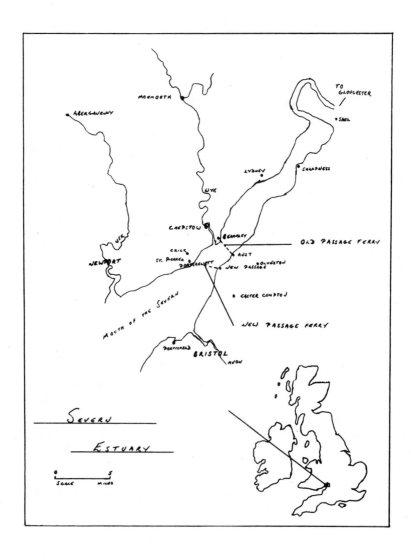

PREFACE

'Aust Ferry'. Not a very evocative name, but as a boy I had often passed the signpost at Cribbs Causeway and wondered quite what form of transport might convey me to that seemingly distant and foreign shore. I don't recall giving it more than passing thought until I was older and decided to cycle to Cardiff as a change from jaunting around North Somerset. On studying the map I quickly saw that, like travellers before me, if I didn't use the ferry I would have a long ride around the Severn estuary via Gloucester. This added a new dimension to my trip and it was with great excitement that I set off from Kenysham to Aust.

I soon discovered that one of the pleasant things about the Old Passage, as it is called, is that you cannot see anything until you arrive at the destination due to the low elevation of the surrounding land. A brisk sou'wester blew me along the coast road but did not augur well for the crossing or my ride to Cardiff. However, snuggled beneath red cliffs beyond I found the offices of the Old Passage Severn Ferry Co. Ltd., complete with an enormous red weighing machine and a rather spartan café. A cup of scalding tea helped to pass the time until the tide rose sufficiently for us to embark.

After a general announcement the by now large convoy of vehicles trundled on to the wooden causeway. Hastening to the tip of the pier I watched the large ferry cautiously drift inwards and be rapidly secured. Safely aboard the *Severn King*, as she was named, I watched the cars negotiate the slippery ramp on to the vessel. The boat was a black and white shallow draughted vessel, oval in shape, with an uncluttered platform deck surmounted by a bridge towards the stern, high on a trestle affair over our heads. There was a large turn-table manoeuvred with ropes by the two nimble deckhands who assisted larger vehicles to squeeze themselves in, making the best use of the space available.

With twin screws rumbling we backed off into the brown tide which caught the vessel and for a moment swept us uncontrollably up stream. A burst of power from engines hidden below sent us cautiously out into the river and heading towards Beachley. The strength of the current was quite apparent from the crab-like manner with which we proceeded over the estuary. By now the keenness of the wind began to kill even my enthusiasm, and I took refuge behind the bridge support with eyes streaming and a cold nose. With surprising rapidity the cliffs of Beachley approached with their crown of green trees. On both banks of the river construction of the new Severn suspension bridge was under way with string-like cables spanning the gap.

Having reached the opposite shore we turned down stream and approached the stone pier. It seemed we had made a rapid passage as another ferry, the *Severn Queen*, was only just departing for Aust. The berth vacated, we took her place alongside and spilled the cars rapidly ashore. As I watched the *Severn King* return the mile or so to the Gloucestershire pier, I gave little consideration to the fact that within a short time this ancient ferry would cease to exist.

Ten years later, I retraced my steps and found the same barren marsh but the rest of the scene had changed. No tubby boats plied back and forth; no row of cars patiently waiting to cross; no longer the pleasant sound of chinking cups as travellers bided their time. Only the boarded up windows, barred doors, chained gates, rotting timbers and decaying piers. Beyond, a steady rumble up stream came from the new Severn Bridge which provided a regular means of passage across the estuary, no longer at the whim of wind and tide.

O River deep and cool
What depths of thought
You urge upon my listening soul.

CONTENTS

LIST OF ILLUSTRATIONS

CHAPTER ONE

Past Events

To today's modern traveller speeding at up to seventy m.p.h. over the Severn Bridge it will be hard to imagine that man ever crossed these broad waters by any other means. A journalist, the late Fred Hando, once said that the greatest gift from St Christopher to travellers over the Severn estuary was Enoch Williams. His enterprise as the founder of the recently closed Old Passage Ferry can only be appreciated if we delve into the distant past and put things into their true perspective.

Historical fact is lost in legend but there is no doubt that an important route of communication lay across the Severn between Beachley and Aust before recorded time. The track way from Avebury divided at Cirencester, one route heading over the hills into South Wales the other pointing towards the red cliffs at Aust.

There is sufficient archeological evidence in the Monmouthshire meadows to build a picture of an established pattern of communities and communications by Roman times between Venta (Caerwent) Isca (Caerleon) and a harbour in the wet lands of Porth-is-coed (Portskewett). A loose translation of the latter is 'harbour below the wood or forest'.

In his book *Roman Roads in Britain*, Ivor Margory highlights the problems modern day historians have in establishing the route of the former Antonine Iter XIV between Caerwent and Bath. His theory is that the Romans measured distance by land miles. This being accepted, a route to Sudbrook from Caerwent, and from a point near Redwick via Over to join with the Gloucester-Sea Mills road, is logical. New Passage was established at a later date roughly on this route but the truth remains a matter of conjecture.

At this time this district probably had closer contacts with the people from across the water, but to the north Offa's Dyke, bisecting Beachley peninsular testifies to contacts of a more violent kind. At the tip of this promontory lies St Tecla's island, surmounted by a beacon now, but crouching beneath its lattice work lie the ruins of a hermit's cell and holy well. St Tecla is said to have been murdered when Christianity was in its infancy. His spirit must lie in the guiding light beaming from the island to present day mariners.

An absence of precise historical evidence on the east shore has led to many traditions as to the origin of the name Aust. The favourite story is associated with St Augustine, seventh century Archbishop of Canterbury. Many places on the Welsh border lay claim to being the meeting place between the Welsh bishops and St Augustine, but Aust has the strongest claim in the opinion of many. Prior to his coming the bishops consulted one of their saintly hermits and asked him whether they should submit to St Augustine. "Certainly, follow him if he is a man of God," he replied.

"How can we find out?" they rejoined.

"Our Lord said, 'Take my yoke upon you and learn of me, for I am meek and lowly in heart'. If therefore Augustine is meek and lowly of heart, believe that he himself has taken the yoke of Christ and is offering it to you; but if he is rude and proud, clearly he is not of God, nor ought you to heed his word."

"But how," they replied, "shall we prove him?"

"Contrive," said the hermit, "that Augustine may come first to the place of meeting, and if he rises to greet you on your arrival, you can know that he is the servant of Christ, and obediently listen to his words; but if he treats you with scorn, and will not rise to greet you, then let him be treated with scorn by you."

The test was duly applied but Augustine unfortunately did not rise to greet them. Further, he denounced many of the customs which they followed as contrary to Catholic tradition. The Welsh bishops therefore refused to comply, and emphatically rejected Roman claims of supremacy, and more particularly Augustine's claim to be their archbishop.

Similarly, the name could equally be a derivation of Augustus after Trajectus Augusti — the ferry of Augustus. Also, Ostorius after Ostorius Scapula, said to have established the route across the Severn for Roman legions to traverse between Caerlon and Silchester.

A writer of 1779, Samuel Rudder speaks of "the tything of Aust, antiently called Austre Clive, because it is situated on the south (Latin auster) cliff of the Severn." A simple but not very romantic explanation.

Actual evidence of the early use of the ferry is sparse but about the year 900 Edward the Elder stood at Aust Clive and Llewellyn, Prince of Wales at Bethersley (Beachley). The latter refused to cross the Severn to the King, so Edward passed over to 'Leoline', 'Who, knowing the King, threw his royal robes on the ground, which he had prepared to sit in judgement with, and leaping breast-high into the water, embracing the boat, said: "Most wise King, your humility has conquered my pride, and your wisdom triumphed over my folly. Mount upon that neck which I so foolishly exalted against you, so shall you enter into that country which your goodness has this day made your own." Then taking him upon his shoulders he made him sit upon his robes and joining hands did him homage.'

In 1131 Winebold de Bolan held the rights from the crown and granted to the abbot and monks of Tintern the right to use the ferry free at 'Auste-Clive'. Further, in 1233/4 Hubert de Burgh, formerly Justiciar to Henry the Third during his minority, fell out of favour when the King came of age and was hotly pursued from Devizes until he escaped with his men and horses. 'For they were able to embark to the last man and horse and tell their pursuers exactly what they thought of them with fingers and thumbs extended'.

John Wycliffe, better known for his translation of the whole Bible from Latin into English held the prebendal stall of Aust in the collegiate church of Westbury-on-Trym from 1362 to 1375. This meant he drew an income from the church which enabled him to continue studies at Oxford but did not mean he held the living. It is thought that he used the ferry route from time to time when visiting the area.

During the reign of Edward the First, William de Mareschal, Earl of Pembroke was granted the right to ferry himself, his servants and his livestock over in his own craft. However at least from the time of Richard the Second the ferry operated as a common law company of unlimited liability with twenty-four shares variously distributed. In 1652 the Manor of Aust came to the family of Sir Samuel Astry, who bought up the shares. At that time twelve boatmen from Aust operated the ferry and it is thought that the landing was to the north of the present bridge. At this spot John Tovey lived at the Old Ferry Inn which was converted later into a house called Tovey's Folly. This has now gone, but the field next to the river at the end of Sandy Lane is still said to be known as 'The Folly'.

During 1645 Charles the First held counsel at Crick House, near Chepstow, the home of the Monmouthshire High Sheriff, Nicholas Moore, and Prince Rupert travelled from Bristol across New Passage to Black Rock at Portskewett to meet him. On 24th July of the same year, again at Crick, Charles heard that Bridgwater had been taken by the rebels and he would be at risk if he went to Bristol. A few Royalists crossed in safety but when the ferryman returned to Black Rock he was pressured into taking a body of Parliament troops in pursuit. Being low tide the English Stones stood high and dry and the passengers were assured that they could walk ashore from there. They soon realized that they were marooned on a reef by the fast rising tide but by then it was too late and all were swept away and drowned. Cromwell was not amused and the ferry was closed; not to be reopened until 1718.

Whilst no ferry was officially permitted it's hard to conceive that the boats ceased entirely to ply for trade between both shores. Supporting this view is the work *Britannia* published by Ogilby in 1689 in which he stated that the road from Bristol to Chester passing through Westbury and Compton to Aust ferry, continued through Chepstow, Monmouth, Hereford, Ludlow, and Shrewsbury to its destination. Later in 1698 he made a detailed sketch of the road from Bristol to Aust, its route passing the gallows on St Michael's Hill through Redland to Westbury village. From there the road passed through Compton and Elberton avoiding the extensive marshes on the coast. *En route* the track followed Cribbs Causeway, a name lost in antiquity, but the present Lamb and Flag inn stands near the site of 'Cribbs', an establishment mentioned on a number of occasions in parochial records. Tom Cribb the pugilist used the causeway as a training ground in the early nineteenth century and this may account for the name.

Prior to this, Jacobus Milerd published a map of Bristol in 1673 with a small inset showing the city and its environs. Many settlements are not shown but it is perhaps indicative of their importance that Beachley and Aust are shown in as great a prominence as the town of Chepstow. Old Passage appears to have been the only route in use at that time since nothing is shown at New Passage, which would be in line with Cromwell's ban, previously mentioned.

In Westbury village a fine finger signpost points the way to the 'Passages' via Channells Hill and the old toll house. Called Dial House after the clock face painted high under the eaves, Mogford relates that the clock is associated with an old tale handed down over the centuries in which the lady of the house was jilted by her suitor at three minutes to twelve and she recorded the fact on the clock face which is still there for us to see today.

A solitary cannon stands duty as a fence-post close to New Passage. Locals say that it came ashore soon after the Roundhead Royalist conflict and is supposed to have some connection with the drowning of Cromwell's troops; a romantic notion but there is no evidence to prove the association.

Fortunately for us John Wesley kept a journal throughout his life and the following are extracts:

'Sunday February 14th 1748. At seven I preached at Bedminster; at Kingswood I began between eight and nine; at Connham (Conham) about two (where I read prayers also) and in Bristol at five. After the society was the love feast, at which my soul was refreshed, but my body was worn out, so that I could hardly speak to be heard; nor did I recover my voice for several days.

'Monday 15th. I set out for Ireland. We came to the New Passage at ten. After waiting about five hours, we found (which they did not care to confess) that the boatmen did not dare to venture out; it blew a storm. We then made to the Old Passage; but the boat was just gone off.

'Tuesday 16th. They talked of passing early; but the storm was too high. I then walked to Aust, where I preached about ten to a small serious congregation. Between four and five, the wind somewhat abating, a boat ventured out and carried us over, we passed through Chepstow, soon after sunset, and pushed on though it got dark, and the untracked snow lay thick upon the ground. About eight we reached the Star, a good, though small, inn, five long miles from Chepstow. It snowed all night.'

Even the most hardened of sceptics must have admired his stamina.

A few years before in October 1743 Charles Wesley had the unpleasant experience of being nearly shipwrecked at New Passage only to hear later that his brother almost suffered the same plight whilst crossing the Trent at the same hour on the same day.

John made many visits to Wales and Ireland and appears to have travelled via New Passage as a matter of course. For example, he states in his journal that he set out on Monday, 19 March 1750 for Ireland via New Passage. Despite a high headwind the crossing was accomplished in less than two hours which appears to have been satisfactory. The scene depicted in J. Hassell's engraving made forty-seven years later must have been quite familiar to both Wesley brothers.

Charles probably recalled their mutual experiences afloat when he wrote the words,

> When, passing through the watery deep,
> I ask in faith His promised aid,
> The waves an aweful distance keep,
> And shrink from my devoted head;
> Fearless their violence I dare;
> They cannot harm, for God is there.

From 1765 the Whitchurch family operated the Old Passage and continued to be associated with the ferry into the next century, John Whitchurch being its first steamboat captain.

A rather macabre story associated with the passages is referred to by Mogford in his history of Westbury-on-Trym. Gibbets were a common sight at this time and a hanging was still a public occasion drawing vast crowds; the body frequently being left to hang in chains for years afterwards.

During 1782 two drovers stole some cattle in Wales and sold them in Bristol. Returning towards the ferry they quarrelled over the division of the money and one, Jenkyns Prothero, murdered his accomplice. He was soon caught and executed after trial, his body being hanged in chains near the junction of what is now Belgrave Road and Pembroke Road, then just a country lane. B. Donne's map of 1826 names the site as Gallows Acre Turnpike: a name which has understandably lapsed from use.

The body became a local attraction and brought crowds of sightseers, increasing business handsomely at the near-by Ostrich Inn. Imaginations were then no less vivid than today and stories of a phantom Jenkyns Prothero walking around the near-by village after the stroke of twelve midnight soon spread. Not unnaturally this unnerved the local residents and permission was obtained to remove the remains which were subsequently buried near the 'White Tree' on the downs. According to *Memoirs of a Gentleman of the Old School* published a while after, some locals could still point out a depression where the body lay.

Prothero was the last criminal to be hanged in chains on the downs but I wonder what today's reaction would be to a spectacle of a dead man hanging as a public exhibit. A doubtful deterrent to the criminal fraternity but I'm sure the curious would still assemble to peer, although perhaps their interest would be a little less open.

Today we still complain about the slowness of road transport and fret at the slightest inconvenience, but a few facts relating to the state of eighteenth century travel might put things in perspective and possibly make us more appreciative of today's communications system.

The *Gloucester Journal* of 27 April 1724 announced that the coaches to Bristol and Bath had begun to 'fly' and would continue for the summer season to perform the journey in ONE day (God permitting). A visit to either town therefore necessitated staying a night away.

During the reign of George I turnpikes began to be established around the country due to the bad state of the roads, and in 1726 Bristol Council sent a petition to Parliament for powers to erect turnpike gates. The Bill was passed in April 1727 but the establishment of the network was only achieved against strong resistance from the local populace, particularly the Kingswood miners. Gates were destroyed, including the Durdham Down Gate. Such outrages continued for at least another ten years and not surprisingly the roads gradually deteriorated beyond their already perilous state.

Matters must have improved for a Bill for the extension of local turnpikes was presented to Parliament in 1758 which contained a proposal to include the road to Aust (the Welsh mail route) which was up a very steep hill (Steep Street) going out of Bristol. It was suggested that a new turnpike road should be made from Frog Lane up what is now Park Street to 'White Ladys Gate' and therefore provide a better route for vehicles travelling to Aust. The Bill became law but nothing was done about the new road until October 1761 when the decision to go ahead with improvements was taken.

Until 1784 a letter sent on Monday from Bristol to London arrived on Wednesday due to the slow system of 'post-boy' deliveries. A local man, John Palmer, proposed to Prime Minister Pitt that the government should establish mail-coaches with armed guards, the extra expense to be offset by the carriage of fare-paying passengers. The Post Office objected to the scheme as a coach system working to a time-table would offer easy pickings for a highwayman. Despite this the scheme was approved and on 2 August 1784 the first mail-coach ran between London and Bristol. Within a few years the system ran nationwide.

CHAPTER TWO

Coaching Days

An announcement dated Saturday 2 October 1802 informed would-be travellers that 'the Union post coach ran from Bristol every Sunday, Wednesday and Friday morning over the Old Passage, through Chepstow and Monmouth to Hereford', where it met other coaches, and returned the day following. All other mails passed via New Passage.

An increase in services in August 1803 to Birmingham, led to a revision in services. The 'Union' coach was noted to depart from the Boar's Head, College Place and alterations were necessary in order 'to render the conveyance as commodious and expeditious as possible' to Sundays, Tuesdays and Thursday mornings at seven o'clock, over the Old Passage, through Chepstow, Monmouth, Abergavenny and Hereford, where it met the Ludlow, Shrewsbury, Chester and Holyhead coaches, and returned the following day and met the Bath, Warminster, Salisbury and Southampton coaches, every Saturday, Tuesday and Thursday mornings at seven o'clock. Performed by W. Williams, Bennett, Whitney, Broome, Young and Co.

The route from Bristol is easily traceable by the modern enthusiast who wishes to relive something of the atmosphere of past days. At one time there was the Whiteladies Gate in Whiteladies Road, Clifton and from here the coach wended its way up Blackboy Hill and over Durdham Downs past the 'White Tree' towards Westbury village. To the right beyond the 'White Tree' stands a defaced 'two miles from Bristol' milestone. Beyond Westbury, Passage Road joins the ancient Cribbs Causeway where the first intact milestone bears the legend, '5 miles to Briftol'. It has a mate just beyond Easter Compton but the others towards Old Passage, at Elinghurst, Redwick, and Aust Pill protrude faceless from the turf.

In 1832 the Postmaster General appointed the engineer Thomas Telford to advise him on ways of improving the mail-coach route between London and Milford Haven to connect with the steam-packets to Ireland. Telford subsequently visited New Passage and surveyed the English Stones reporting it as 'One of the most forbidding places at which an important ferry was ever established, a succession of violent cataracts formed in a rocky channel exposed to the rapid rush of a tide which has scarcely an equal on any other coast'. Hardly a recommendation. He thought the longer passage between Uphill and Sully Island a safer alternative even though an additional twenty-two miles of road would have to be constructed. The Postmaster General disagreed and Telford took a closer look at the Aust to Beachley route. As the narrowest point on the estuary it was an obvious choice and with commendable foresight Telford proposed a suspension bridge to fill the gap, but nothing came of this plan.

The only tangible evidence we have today of his presence lies in the work of his assistant, Henry Habberley Price, who supervised the construction of stone piers at Beachley and Aust. A contemporary newspaper report stated 'It is found practicable, without materially increasing the expense, to extend the width of the pier (Beachley) to 30 feet, which will secure a convenient embarkation and landing to the most timid'. One presumes that potential customers had previously been put off by the unsafe condition of the pier.

Until this period sailing vessels continued to provide an uncertain ferry at the whim of wind and tide which did not really fit the time schedules of the Royal Mail, but, during 1825 the Old Passage Ferry Association met and agreed to consider the purchase of a steamboat. I imagine some pressure was being exerted by the Postmaster General but the significance of their decision should be noted, as only thirteen years before Henry Bell had launched his *Comet* on the Clyde, the first commercial steamboat on Britain's waters. At the time the prospect of belching clouds of black smoke and hot sparks deterred potential operators but for European shipping a new era had dawned. With the end of the Napoleonic wars there was a boom in the production of steamboats, all paddle powered. Time was to prove that paddles were not particularly suitable as a means of propulsion in deep sea but were well suited to estuary and river where, with a shallow draught hull, they could be fast, manoeuvrable and relatively economical to run, despite the primitive engines available during those early years.

1836 saw Francis Smith patenting the screw propeller but it is noticeable that all Severn steam-ferries in the nineteenth century continued to be paddle-powered.

Rather than opt for the expense of buying a steamboat it was suggested by the association that one way of stimulating trade was to buy up the New Passage and thus have a monopoly of the traffic! Not surprisingly this suggestion brought a hostile response from the rival company, and by the end of the year a new steamboat, the *St Pierre* was plying the New Passage. She was the first steam vessel built at Newport and only weighed thirty tons but had a cabin and 'sloop rig'. She was named after the near-by manor whose Lord had held the ferry rights from centuries past. Business prospered with the mail contracts bringing a regular income.

From 1771 to 1832 Lieutenant Colonel Daniel Paterson published an annual handbook for travellers of the time, which noted that at New Passage it cost twelve shillings to carry across a four-wheeled carriage; a shilling for a two-wheeled carriage; a shilling per horse and one shilling and sixpence a horse and rider; pedestrians ninepence, cattle sixpence a head; sheep, pigs and lambs three shillings and fourpence per score. For those who could afford it a small boat could be hired to take you across for five shillings and ninepence for every passenger you took with you. By 1832 the fee had increased to six shillings and one shilling respectively. Considering contemporary money values the ferry was expensive but it could be argued that so was every form of freight at this period.

Even after the opening of the Severn Railway Tunnel later in the century livestock continued to be transported by sea to and from Chepstow market. Old Passage House at Aust was an hostelry at one time and it was the practice for farmers and drovers to drive their livestock to the pens at the bottom of the hill and adjourn to the house for refreshment and accommodation when waiting for the tide.

At one time the house was gabled and the attic rooms were traditionally known in the Alway family as the 'Irish Rooms' where dealers slept on their way to and from Bristol markets. Today it is a private residence. It is also a tradition that sailing craft would beach on Aust Wharf and discharge large numbers of cattle from Ireland destined for West Country slaughter-houses. Races too took place on the wharf; a signal post once standing in the grounds of Old Passage House being used to start the scratch competitions on the rough turf.

The rival Old Passage Ferry Association quickly challenged the operations of the *St Pierre* by erecting a new 486 foot long pier at Aust in 1826 and introducing a steam ferry soon after. Competition was fierce but by 1831 all mail went via Old Passage; the *St Pierre* being sold to a Mr Price at Neath Abbey and subsequently converted into a sailing craft in 1841.

This domination was not acquired without a fight. *Felix Farley's Journal* tells its own story.

'Milford and Brecknock Mail Coach

A coach sets out from the White Hart, Broad Street, Bristol, over the Old Passage (Aust) every Sunday, Wednesday, and Friday at noon, and joins the above coach at Ragland the same day; and a corresponding coach returns from Milford on certain days.' The punchline followed 'N.B. This road is nineteen miles nearer to Carmarthen and Milford than the lower one.' — that is, by the New Passage. The White Hart and its neighbour, the White Lion later became the Grand Hotel.

Not unnaturally, there was a hot response, given in the following advertisement: 'A CAUTION — The public will please observe that no other mail coach whatever does now, or ever has, run from Bristol to Milford Haven, excepting the Royal London, Bath, Bristol, and Milford Haven mail coach, which sets out from the Bush Inn and Tavern Corn Street, every Monday, Tuesday, Thursday, and Saturday, and the mail coach to Swansea every day from the same inn, notwithstanding the flaming advertisement of a certain set of men to deceive and mislead the public, by their asserting that the road over the Old Passage is nineteen miles nearer than over the New Passage, which is so far from being a fact that the road of the New Passage is seven and three-quarters nearer, as was proved by admeasurement by orders of the office, making a difference of twenty-six miles and three-quarters nearer the lower (that is, the New Passage) than the upper road.'

A detailed reply by the Old Passage proprietors is interesting for a comparison of routes from Bristol.

Upper Road	Miles	Lower Road	Miles
Old Passage	11	New Passage	10
Across the Water	1	Across the Water	3
Raglan	14	Newport	15
Abergavenny	9	Cardiff	12
Brecknock	19	Cowbridge	12
Trecastle	10	Pill	12
Llandovery	9	Neath	13
Llandeilo	12	Pontardulais	10
Carmarthen	15	Carmarthen	9
St Clears	9	St Clears	9
Narberth	13	Narberth	13
Haverford-West	10	Haverford-West	10
Milford	10	Milford	10
Total	142	Total	161

'In favour of the Upper Road, 19 miles.'

Every success has a price and a letter addressed to a Mrs John York of Olveston dated Chepstow, 15 March 1830 tells its own story.

The Old Passage Ferry Association Secretary J.A. Evans wrote:

'I am directed to call your serious attention to the present state of the Old Passage Ferry Association.

'At a General Meeting of the Proprietors on the 4th of February last, it appeared that the existing debts amount to £7,201.14.4 of which £4,500 is secured on mortgage of the Inns, Steam Packet & Co. and that for the residue, amounting to £2,701.14.4. due as per annexed Statement to sundry Creditors the Shareholders are each, separately as well as jointly, liable.

'That the Creditors had began to get very uneasy, and had threatened Proceedings against certain of the Proprietors.

'That there is no prospect of continuing the Association, especially as a large sum of money is now absolutely necessary for the Repairs of the Inns & Co. That to pay off the mortgage, and meet these debts and payments, it would require an advance of at least £40 upon each share.

'It was therefore resolved to submit to the Proprietors, whether it would not be better to request the mortgagees to take on the Concern as it stands at the present moment, subject to the whole amount of Debts.

'Under all the circumstances, the Directors have arrived at the determination to call once more a General Meeting, to take into consideration the dissolving of the Association, according to the Deed of Regulations: and if they should fail in finding on that day a sufficient number of Proprietors to carry on the business, and bring it to a determined issue, they must resign an office which they feel they can no longer retain with hope of benefit to the Association.

'The General Meeting is fixed for Wednesday the 24th of March instant, at the Beaufort Arms Inn, Chepstow, at Twelve o'clock at noon, at which your attendance is earnestly solicited.'

The result of this meeting I do not know but the ferry continued. Two of the principal creditors were James Jenkins and Oliver Chapman, both trustees of the association, who were owed £155 and £66.5.1 respectively, therefore it was in the interest of both of them to see the Association thrive. The latter had considerable local standing as a large shipowner and ship builder so no doubt he exercised some influence on the decision to continue.

The first steamboat on Old Passage was the *Worcester*, built by William Scott at Bristol and delivered in March 1827. Ferry rights were owned by the Duke of Beaufort and he and several Chepstow merchants backed the Old Passage Ferry Association. Services commenced on 13 June 1827 but the *Worcester* came to a spectactular end when she accidentally caught alight and burnt to the water line. Her few remains were purchased by a Lydney man who rebuilt her as a schooner. She survived until 1891 when she went down off the Glamorgan coast. Prior to the accident a second vessel called *Beaufort* had been acquired by a further consortium and put into use in 1832. A second *Worcester* entered service in 1838, with the *Beaufort* as stand-by although attempts were made to sell her.

Felix Farley's Journal of June 1836 noted that, 'The two sons of the Prince of Orange and their retinue crossed the Severn at Old Passage Ferry on Thursday and after expressing their satisfaction at the attention paid them by the superintendent and boatmen, they ordered dinner at the Beachley Inn.'

Other people had a different view of the service provided. Nicholson's Cambrian Travellers' Guide of 1840 itemized the expense of crossing without comment but was scathing of the service provided. He noted the monopoly of both Old and New Passage as the gateway to Monmouthshire from the South West and regarded such an arrangement as contrary to public interest. To quote, 'The boatmen are, of course, rude in their manners, indifferent to the accommodation of the passengers and practised in the arts of extortion.' An additional warning followed, 'If the traveller be necessitated to pass over the ferry at low water, he will have to disembark at a short distance from the usual landing place and be subjected to a very slippery walk over the surface of rock covered with Confervae, Fuce and other marine plants.' Hardly a recommendation for future customers.

A local resident of the time, Oliver Norris, recalled that as the coach wended its way through Pilning and Northwick to Old Passage, people would hand up a penny and a letter to the mail guard in a cleft stick as it passed by, but if the penny was missing the letter was thrown away. The Royal Mail was no charity.

We are told that by 1836 the stage coach services in this country had reached their zenith, the growth of the railways leading to their disappearance within a short number of years. A résumé of services provided in that year has been compiled by Alan Bates which would seem to indicate that the London-Bristol-Pembroke Royal Mail operated by Chaplin & Co. reverted to New Passage by that time. Pembroke Dock replaced Milford as the Irish Packet Port from 1836. Some idea of the gruelling nature of long distance travel in those days can be gauged from the fact that the coach left the Swan with Two Necks at Lad Lane, London at 7.30 p.m. and arrived at, I think, Coopers Office, 6 High Street, Bristol at 7.45 a.m. the next morning. Fifteen minutes later the coach left for New Passage, a journey scheduled to take one hour twelve minutes. The journey then continued via Cardiff to Swansea to arrive at Pembroke at 1.09 a.m. the following day, a total travelling time of twenty-nine hours thirty-nine minutes. When you consider that most coaches carried four inside and eleven on top it is no wonder that travelling at that time was always done out of necessity rather than pleasure.

At this time W. Jones & Co. and J. Edwards & Co. operated rival services Monday to Saturday from Bristol to Brecon, and J. Niblett & Co. operated a similar service from Bristol to Hereford. I presume all were via Old Passage. The latter operated 'The Monarch' London to Bristol coach which terminated at the White Hart and White Lion, Broad Street, Bristol so it is probable the services were connected. Several routes radiated from Hereford and it was possible to obtain connections to Holyhead from there. Within the old city wall at Bristol coaches terminated at the hotels mentioned and also at the Rummer Hotel and the Bush, Corn Street. A considerable traffic passed through between the Midlands and West Country and there must have been a large movement of people changing here to travel across the Severn via the passages and save the journey by way of Gloucester.

Long distance passenger traffic by road declined rapidly as the railways expanded but two accidents on the Severn did little to help sustain trade on the passages. During 1839 the sailing packet *Jane* was lost in a gale on the Benches with all hands, then on 30 March 1855 a further catastrophe occurred. Various versions of the tale exist but confirmation of the accident lies on a tomb in Aust churchyard to the memory of George Pendock who perished with six others on the Severn ferry boat. The story goes that the sailing vessel *Despatch* was heavily loaded after a day of transactions at Chepstow market and had twenty sheep, thirty-six pigs, five oxen, one horse and a number of passengers on board. Approaching Aust a squall blew up and threw the vessel on to some wooden piles with disastrous results: seven were drowned and one person came ashore at Severn Beach after hanging on to the tail of a cow! One variation states that a total of seven lives were saved but whatever the truth the scenes of confusion and distress are not hard to imagine.

A vessel *Dispatch* was built by Patterson and Mercer at Bristol in 1831. If this was the vessel concerned she normally served on the Bristol to Chepstow service and despite the accident continued to trade until 1870.

Tragedy struck again on Monday 13 September 1869. Mr Doulton, Landlord of the Llandoger Inn, King Street, Bristol also acted as a tugboat agent and on that fateful day received instruction to send the tug *Old Forager* to Gloucester. She had been built in 1826 as a wooden paddler but was altered to the role of screw-driven tug by John Payne of Bristol in 1862. Being unable to secure the services of a Captain, Doulton took the vessel himself but between New and Old Passage she was struck by 'an exceptionally strong storm' and literally 'hit to pieces' after bumping the shallows for four miles. The crew clung to wreckage when the vessel broke up but her temporary master chose to swim for the shore. Had he remained with his men he, like they, would probably have been rescued but this was not to be and his body was washed ashore at Avonmouth.

CHAPTER THREE

Railway Interlude

During 1845 the South Wales Union Railway sought to establish a rail-link across the Severn, and by Act of Parliament the following year, acquired the ferry rights of the Old and New Passage and the right to lay a railway connection to both routes. The Old Passage was purchased for £30,000 which gives some idea of its importance as a mail-route at this time. Despite good intentions nothing happened and the company was wound up in October 1853.

The following year a Select Committee was appointed to look into ways of improving the regularity of carrying mail by rail. Mr F.G. Saunders, Secretary of the South Wales Railway gave evidence of the frequent loss of time to the South Wales night mail caused by late receipt of the Bristol and West of England mails at Chepstow via the Old Passage Ferry. I presume that the ferry had reverted to sail power and its regularity had deteriorated accordingly. One of the results of the inquiry was that future mails were sent via Gloucester, a longer distance but at least they arrived with greater punctuality. The Bristol and Gloucester Railway had opened on 8 July 1844 and the 'Bush' coach office was closed in March the same year, its trade having dwindled away.

In 1854 a further attempt to form a new company to run from New Passage was made but again fizzled out. 1857 saw a new Act passed and construction commenced in October 1858. A short connection was made with the South Wales Railway at Portskewett via a deep cutting, the line travelling out to sea on

OPENING OF THE BRISTOL AND SOUTH WALES UNION RAILWAY AND FERRY : NEW PASSAGE HOTEL AND PIER

Opening of the Bristol & South Wales Union Railway & Ferry: New Passage Hotel & Pier, 25th August 1863. Passengers transferred from the train to the ferry boat which took them across the Severn to Portskewett Pier where another train took them into Wales.

a pier 708 feet long from Black Rock into deep water where stairs led passengers down to a pontoon at the extremity. Two miles away a similar arrangement 1,635 feet long connected with the shore at New Passage. From there the broad-gauge line extended to South Wales Junction at Bristol, eleven and a half miles away by way of an enormous cutting at Horfield and a lengthy tunnel at Patchway. A hotel was built at each end of the crossing to accommodate travellers waiting to cross. Due to vagaries of wind and tide both hotels proved to be a profitable investment. The *Illustrated London News* gave the official opening on 25 August 1863 a detailed coverage, in particular the benefits to the public of the new service. The distance between Bristol and Cardiff through Gloucester was ninety-four miles by rail. This was now reduced to thirty-eight.

The report continued, 'The piers at the Severn, undoubtedly the most interesting works on the line, are formed of creosoted timber, and the construction of both piers is the same, with the exception of the foundations, which, on the New Passage side, consists of piles driven firmly into the ground till they reach the rock below, which exists at a depth of from 6ft to 20ft. The superstructure is carried on upright timbers, braced together in couples, and standing in rows of five couples. There are upwards of seventy rows, which are 22ft apart, and connected at the top by longitudinal balks corresponding with the uprights, on which five-inch planking is laid transversely, and which carries the permanent way. The pier is erected to a height of 50ft above low-water mark.'

At Portskewett some difficulty was experienced in establishing the pier because of the rocky shore but masonry foundations with cast iron shoes to contain the piles solved the problem. Opening was delayed but the complete Portskewett branch was opened on 1 January 1864.

At the official opening the Mayors of Bristol, Newport and Cardiff were entertained by Herr Pfeiffers' Bristol Volunteer Artillery Band but the day was damp and dismal and gave an indication of what future passengers could expect.

Two paddle-steam ferry boats the *Gem* and *Relief* opened the service with the first crossings commencing on 7 September and the public being admitted the following day. A small vessel called the *Dragon Fly* is thought to have acted as a

Beachley Passage House — an engraving by J. Hassell, London 1797. A couple wait with their packhorses and cow for the gangway to be wheeled from beneath the cliff.

Courtesy Newport Museum and Art Gallery

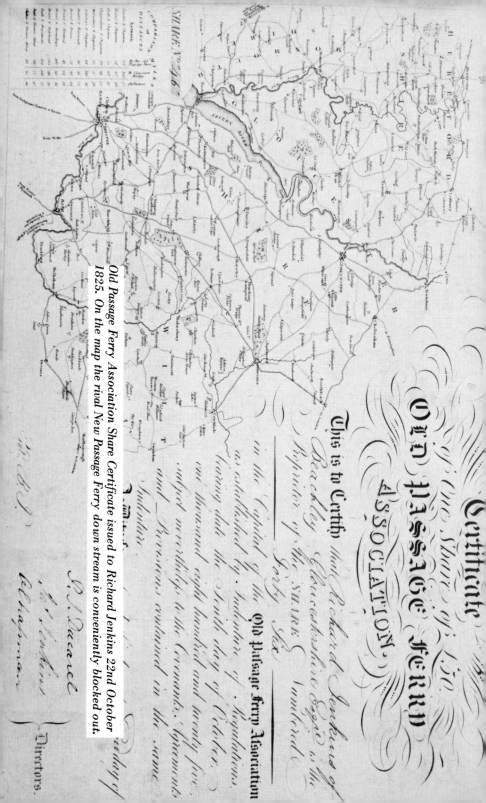

Old Passage Ferry Association Share Certificate issued to Richard Jenkins 22nd October 1825. On the map the rival New Passage Ferry down stream is conveniently blocked out.

Paddle Steamer Beaufort, of the Old Passage Ferry Association, passing Rownham Ferry on the river Avon, Hotwells, Bristol. Named after the Duke of Beaufort she was built at Chepstow in 1832.
Artist unknown
Courtesy Bristol City Museum and Art Gallery

New Passage House by J. Hassell. Passage to Black Rock, Portskewett cost a shilling for a horse and ninepence for its rider. The ferry boat beyond appears to have a sprit rigged main and working mizzen masts.

Courtesy Newport Museum and Art Gallery

Company Seal of the Bristol & South Wales Union Railway. *Courtesy Swindon Museum*

Steam Tug President, later used at New Passage, acting as tender to the passenger vessel President in the Mersey 1839. A contemporary of the Great Western, the larger President was built for the British & American Steam Navigation Co. only to founder with all 135 souls on her second voyage. Painting by Samuel Walters

Courtesy Merseyside County Museums

New Passage Ferry the Gem after her return to the Mersey. The funnel lies across the open after-deck after striking the Bowfell on 26th November 1878. Fifteen died.   *Courtesy Wallasey Public Libraries*

Tragedy again, a much modified Gem wrecked on Porthlow Beach, Isles of Scilly, 21st November 1881 en route to West Africa. All machinery appears to have been torn out or salvaged.
    Courtesy Gibson Isles of Scilly

Iron Paddle-steamer Christopher Thomas named after the chairman of the Bristol & South Wales Union Railway. Still an open bridge but a large saloon made her a popular cruising vessel even after the ferry closed.

Courtesy Grahame Farr

*rial run at Beachley, July 1926. Convalescent boys from Beachley amp along for the ride aboard the Silver Queen.
Geof. Blatchford and Horace Olney (L and R) at the tiller.*

First car, Beachley July 1926. Bob Treherne between the Olney Brothers pose before hoisting the Williams' Gwynne 8 aboard the Silver Queen for the passage to Aust. The car was produced by The Gwynnes Engineering Co., Chiswick 1922-25.

Unofficial cargo. Beachley 1926, under customer pressure the odd small car was taken across at owner's risk. *Courtesy J. Ross*

Legal passengers wait to board with bicycles and motor bikes. Officers from Beachley camp look on.

Courtesy J. Ross

Half models of the first two car ferries. (Top) Princess Ida, note pleasing lines of the wooden hull in contrast to the rotund body of the steel Severn Queen, (Bottom), built with greater capacity in mind. It is probable that the Ida was built from this model.

Courtesy John Williams

Princess Ida takes shape in the hands of Hurd and Henderson on the banks of the Wye, Chepstow. The oak stem came from Sedbury Park. The deck sections for the Severn Bridge and gates for West Dock went down the same slip later.

Launching Ceremony. Mrs Ida Williams christening her namesake.

Afloat her shallow draught can be gauged from the figures on the bows.

Inauguration 31st July 1931. Enoch Williams' Singer car stands precariously on two planks. Builders Hurd, first left and Henderson, third left, aboard the Ida.

IDA

Paying passengers August 1931. Note stove pipe chimney and open bridge. Launch May Queen in foreground.

Beachley Pier 1931. Cars wait to board the Princess Ida.

"The Old Passage Severn, Beachley"

...owed on 21st ... on February 1934. Bob Jones, engineer (with pipe) contemplates her plight. Note addition of funnel and wheelhouse.

GEM AFTER N. HOPPS.

company hack for carrying crew, supplies and accessories. Both ferry boats sported the company colours of red bands on their black funnels.

The *Gem* started life as the brain-child of a nephew of the Coulbourn brothers, joint proprietors of the Egremont and New Brighton Ferries on the River Mersey. She was launched as the *Liscard* in 1858 by James Napier at Govan. She was said to have been of 'unusual' build and not very successful. Cabins were provided below deck, apparently without portholes. I presume decklights were provided but the accommodation must have been dungeon-like. She was certified to carry 417 passengers most of whom probably preferred to stay on the windswept deck. She continued in service until 1861 when under the Wallasey Improvement Act of 1861 the Wallasey Local Board purchased the Coulbourns' business. Some rebuilding had given her an excuse for a change of name, Liscard being one of the swallowed up villages from which Wallasey was formed. After resuming service as the *Gem* she was sold abroad but not delivered. Instead she reverted to a member of the Coulbourn family and was registered in Glasgow.

What service she performed in the intervening years I cannot establish but in June 1863 she was purchased by the Bristol and South Wales Union Railway Company and delivered to Bristol on 6th July. Her service at New Passage must have been no happier than further north for the following year saw her repurchased by the Wallasey Board from Mark Whitworth (Whitwell?) & Sons of Bristol for £1,050 and later given a re-engining and rebuild.

On 26 November 1878 she was to figure in the greatest tragedy ever to occur on the Mersey ferry service. She left

PORTSKEWETT PIER.
(WITH THE WORKS - SUDBROOK IN THE BACKGROUND)

Portskewett Pier. Paddle steamer Chepstow crossing from New Passage. After the 1881 fire, passengers had to walk to the pier-head to catch the train.

Courtesy Kingsmead Reprints

Seacombe at about 9.30 a.m. with 250 passengers on board. A dense fog covered the river and the vessel headed blindly across the flood tide. Anchored in mid-river was the Brocklebank sailing vessel *Bowfell*. The *Gem* passed beneath her bowsprit but her funnel was dislodged and fell to the deck amongst the throng of passengers. With the tremendous crash and the probable clouds of dirty smoke mingling with the swirling fog the uproar and confusion must have been frightening. In the panic some people were pushed overboard and a total of fifteen lives were lost. One can only be thankful that no such tragedy ever happened at New Passage.

Soon after she was sold for service in West Africa but got no further than the Isles of Scilly for, whilst anchored in St Mary's Pool, she was subjected to a strong gale which blew her ashore at Porthlow on 21 November, 1881.

Her sister the *Relief* was more successful. She was newly in service with the New Steam Tug Co. of Liverpool in 1862 and spent her first few months at New Passage on approval. She was purchased outright on 11 September 1863 and continued uneventfully in service until June 1874 when she went to Liverpool as the *Mersey King* to become a tug and excursion vessel.

A wooden paddle-tug the *President* also arrived in 1863 but she was well past her prime having first served on the Mersey as a passenger vessel and later on the Lougher in South Wales as a tug. An artist by the name of Samuel Walters featured the vessel in the foreground of a painting of a larger steamship of the same name. Whether she acted as a regular ferry is unknown but her wooden hull was broken up two years later.

Service improved when the purpose built *Christopher Thomas* arrived on 26 June 1864, named after the company chairman. She had good catering arrangements and was frequently used for excursions; for example, a one shilling trip to view H.M.S. *Defiance* at anchor in Walton Bay was very popular, with special excursion trains laid on from Bristol to connect with the boat at New Passage.

The Great Western Railway were keen to improve communications with South Wales and purchased the Bristol and South Wales Union Railway on August 1868. *Christopher Thomas* must have been a satisfactory vessel for the new owners ordered a new vessel from her makers, Henderson, Coulbourn & Co. of Renfrew to be named *Chepstow*. She was delivered in June 1875 and featured twin funnels.

The late Archie Powell of Bristol Newspaper fame started his working career as a steward and cabin boy on the *Christopher Thomas* and recalled that she and her companion the *Chepstow* were crowded at holiday times, with a German street band from Bristol giving inspiration to the festive air. The New Passage Hotel provided shrimp teas whilst the evenings would be spent in the elegant Long Room dancing or enjoying a sing-song to a piano accompaniment.

In line with the change of gauge on the Great Western the Portskewett branch was converted to standard between 11 and 13 May 1872 and the Gloucestershire section between 7th and 9th August the following year.

Portskewett Pier suffered considerable fire damage on the night of 23 May 1881 but escaped complete destruction due to the prompt action of the nightwatchman at New Passage. He rowed a hastily summoned crew to the *Christopher Thomas* who then proceeded smartly across the river and helped to extinguish the blaze by pumping water from the river on to the lift and pontoon, which were found to have been severely damaged and unusable. The next day the *Christopher Thomas* took a train-load of passengers from New Passage to Chepstow, but this was no solution due to tidal difficulties playing havoc with the existing timetable. Repairs took longer than expected but traffic resumed on 16th June. As can be seen on the illustration of Portskewett the train used to reverse on to the pier, but after the fire this practice was discontinued and all traffic boarded or alighted at a temporary platform built below the Black Rock Hotel.

Despite the relative efficiency of the ferry it was obvious that if a crossing could be effected without a change in the mode of transport then industrialists and travellers in general would be eternally grateful. Several grandiose schemes were mooted for building larger bridges but these came to naught due to the technical problems rather than the relatively short distance involved. Up stream, the Severn and Wye and Severn Bridge Railway Company built a railway bridge between Gatcombe and Sharpness, commencing in 1875 and opening in October

1879. Following the fire at Portskewett, trains were diverted around this single track bridge for a short while. Nearer home Charles Richardson deposited plans in Parliament in November 1871 for a four and a half mile tunnel to run from Sudbrook to a point south of New Passage. The Act was passed the following year and work commenced in 1873. The initial difficulty was expected to be tunnelling under 'The Shoots', a trench in the river bed, but the greatest problem was an underground river draining the surrounding hills which constantly flooded the workings. Thomas Walker in his book *The Severn Tunnel* gives an accurate account of the incredible difficulties they faced in its making which, despite its factual approach, reads like a thriller. Even in adversity there were lighter moments such as when a dormitory chimney at New Passage situated in a weak spot on the line of the tunnel disappeared suddenly into the bowels of the earth, much to the consternation of the inmates of the hut! Fortunately there were no casualties. 1 December 1886 saw the tunnel opened with the *Christopher Thomas* making the last crossing that day. Both she and the *Chepstow* carried on the excursion trips for a while longer but were sold to a Cardiff timber merchant in 1890. Like the *Gem, Christopher Thomas* ended up sold to West African buyers but managed to get there intact and gave a few years useful service before stranding *en route* to becoming a breakwater in 1902 when her active life was finished. Renamed *Rover* the *Chepstow* was wrecked near Youghal in July 1899.

To most people of that time it was thought that the Severn Tunnel and the bridge up stream provided a complete answer to the transport problem across the Severn and the ferries were neglected. Further down the estuary the Somerset and Dorset Railway ran a service between Burnham and Cardiff, on and off between 1858 and 1888 but the passenger traffic was sporadic and reduced to freight only from Highbridge Wharf until the winding up of the S. & D. shipping affairs.

I have no doubt that boats could still be hired from Chepstow for a while but by the turn of the century the ferry had become only a memory.

Communications of a different sort saw pioneer work done on the banks of the Severn by Harry Grindell Matthews, a man of immense foresight and grasp of technical detail. Born at

Winterbourne Court, Gloucestershire on St Patrick's Day, 17 March 1880 he showed an early interest in the problems associated with the transmission of speech and sound and this was fostered later at the Merchant Venturer's School in Bristol. At sixteen he was apprenticed to an electrical firm for three years but because of his grasp of the subject was able to cancel his indentures after only eighteen months. He served later in the Boer War and after being invalided home he became consulting engineer to Lord de la Warr on his estate at Bexhill-on-Sea. By this time wireless-telephone and its problems had become an obsession with 'G.M.', as he was known, and he was soon to prove the possibility of wireless communication. During 1910 the Aerophone and its potential became public knowledge and his achievement was widely acclaimed, being elected a member of the Royal Institute. Shortly after he moved to Black Rock at Portskewett where he established a radio station with a small band of assistants.

An amusing incident at this station became a historic occasion for it witnessed the first broadcast. On leaving the lodgings of a Miss Foster one of the assistants instructed her to switch on a little black box at midday which they had left with her. On the stroke of twelve, across five and a half miles a little ditty came through the box loud and clear to the consternation of both landlady and maid. It said,

> This birthday message comes through space
> To greet you, bless your pretty face,
> With every wish for happiness,
> And best of luck by wireless.

The maid thought it was a voice from Mars!

In January 1912 the Black Rock laboratory had the whole of the press agog. An alert newspaper reporter overheard two men discussing a mysterious voice picked up on a morse headset by a ship's radio officer on passage between Avonmouth and Hamburg. Besides a few words a popular tune, 'Two eyes of grey', was heard on this and subsequent transmissions. The astonishing factor was that people 600 miles apart picked up the message which soon became dubbed the 'North Sea Ghost'. Anonymity was maintained until a company falsely claimed credit for the messages and G.M. decided it was time to reveal all. At Buckingham Palace on 4,

July 1912, the Royal Family was given a demonstration of the Grindell Matthews apparatus, the future King Edward VIII and King George VI talking to their mother whilst sitting in separate cars in different places in the grounds. Soon after Lloyd George also had a demonstration but enthusiasm by the home government was lukewarm and G.M. looked to France for support. Events were overtaken by the declaration of war and for some unknown reason his broadcasting stations were placed under lock and key, he being denied access to his workshops. By the time peace came developments had rendered his equipment out of date and he had meanwhile turned his energies elsewhere.

Discussions with Lord Fisher, First Sea Lord, led to experiments on the Severn to improve the method of locating German U-Boats which were having a one-sided war to the detriment of British shipping. Existing hydrophone equipment was found wanting and G.M. reasoned that as every motor generates its own magnetic field then some electrical device could no doubt be invented to locate it.

Initially tests with a submarine were based at Portsmouth but with so much conflicting traffic it was decided to move to the relative peace of the Severn. A motor boat towing a submerged motor gave promising results and the services of a steam drifter, the *Sea Queen*, and a tug, the *Volunteer*, were obtained to scale up the experiment. Trials at New Passage culminated in a demonstration in which the observers were able to see that the equipment on the *Sea Queen* was able to hear clearly a two horse power motor on the *Volunteer*. Following this trials were moved to Barry.

After the war G.M. moved to Pilning and turned his attention to more peaceful experiments. One of the problems of the early film industry was that speech was normally relayed by gramophone record with all the attendant difficulties of synchronization to give it credibility; the upshot being that no attempt was made to improve the realism of the moving picture, sub-titles being quite the norm.

With the aid of his chief assistant, Lynes, they began experiments in the ballroom of the New Passage Hotel. Equipment was set up in the ballroom and in a room adjoining across the hallway separated by glass doors. A quote from

Barwell's, *The death ray man*, tells the rest of the story.

'The microphone was in circuit with a specially wound transformer and a battery; the other side of the transformer was in series with an Edison battery supplying the 10-ampere arc light. The lamp projected a beam across the hall (from the small room) through on to a small mirror, which in turn, bent the ray along the length of the ballroom to a small parabolic mirror, focused to throw a spot of light, about the size of a shilling, on to a selenium bridge. This bridge was connected in series with a battery and with the input of a two stage Browne telephone relay, and the output was transferred to a loud speaker. A gramophone was played in front of the distant microphone, initiating a series of rather wonderful happenings. The vibration of the voice on the gramophone record were changed to electric, and then to light, waves; the operating beam of light coming through the two glass doors was reflected by the first mirror on to the second, which in turn, condensed and reflected it on the selenium bridge; its vibrations were electric, then in the telephone relay, changed to sound vibration. The loud speaker amplified these, and the process was complete.'

I feel sure that the ferry travellers of a few years previous would have been startled with the notion that their conversation could be transmitted by a beam of light but this was in fact so. Unfortunately G.M. faced considerable opposition to his discovery both here and in America, it being a well-known fact that many 'silent' stars had no voice worth listening to and thus too many fortunes were at stake. Patents were not renewed and for this slip G.M. was to be sorry for in a short while 'talkies' swept the world.

In later years he and his colleagues experimented with the so-called 'death ray' which was in effect a concentration of immense electrical energy at a given point which was then focused on a particular spot in a similiar manner to the modern laser beam. Plate glass could be melted, gunpowder ignited and engines stopped by this invisible force. Vermin were killed at a distance of sixty-four feet, so its sinister potential was quickly appreciated. Later it was established that the beam could operate over a distance of several miles and I'm told that in one experiment the equipment was able to stop a lorry engine situated on the opposite bank of the Severn from New Passage.

Development faded into obscurity in later years but to his dying day Grindell Matthews maintained that his death ray had a more useful purpose than that to which the public mind readily applied it.

I have only mentioned here the events in his life relevant to our tale but I think he notes a higher place in English history than the complete obscurity into which he has sunk today.

A pleasant day can be had visiting New Passage on both sides of the river and exploring the remains such as they are.

On the Welsh side the cutting from the main line is easily followed as it curves beneath the road and points out to sea. Placed at periodic intervals are G.W.R. boundary markers with one despondent specimen standing forlorn above the waves. In 1873 Portskewett parish was reported to be of agricultural aspect and possessing 260 souls. At Black Rock, beside the hotel there were three or four cottages, occupied by the inspector of the steamboat pier, and other railway staff. The hotel is now a private house with a few outbuildings leading to a stone slip, but looking across at the white shape of New Passage Hotel it is easy to picture that inspector raising the alarm when his pier was on fire and the desperate attempts to put it out that followed. Today, Black Rock is a lonely spot with only its memories for company. In complete contrast, the urbanization of near-by villages has meant a considerable increase in the number of visitors to the site of the ferry on the east shore. A modern sea wall provides an excellent if bracing walk from Severn Beach but I often wonder how many bother to dwell on the business that existed here less than a hundred years ago. The course of the railway is easily defined but overgrown, whilst the New Passage Hotel has a timeless elegance all its own. A stumpy stone pier stands hacked off at the water's edge, a forlorn reminder of the massive timber structure that once extended finger like towards the opposite shore. No longer can we hear the hiss and clank of simmering locomotives and the banging of carriage doors, only the laughter of children and barking of dogs oblivious of the past.

CHAPTER FOUR

A New Era

Two years after the opening of the Severn Tunnel, Llansamlet near Swansea saw the birth of Enoch Williams in March 1888 to the village grocer, John Rees Williams, and his wife, Anne, née Richards. He grew up in sight and sound of the sea and used the halfpenny ferry across the Towey to go to school. Half-day holidays were often spent exploring Swansea Docks. With the chance of a trip in a tug or pilot boat. Later he went to Swansea Grammar School and was able to benefit from having the father of Dylan Thomas as a history master. On leaving school his father dispelled his son's seaborne notions and he was articled to a Swansea Architect for five years. At the end of this time he took his finals and became an associate of the Royal Institute of British Architects. When working in Cardiff he met Miss Ida Matthews, daughter of John Bissie Matthews, a Norton St. Phillip farmer, who was employed as a milliner in the days when every hat was an individual creation. They were married on 29 July 1914 and as Enoch told me, 'War broke out!'

Service with the Royal Engineers led to him joining a team who planned the ammunition train ferry from Richborough to Dieppe, Calais and Dunkirk. Peace brought a return to Cardiff but 1920 saw the opportunity of advancement and he became Chief Architectural Assistant at Newport. Successfully appointed he applied for a similar position later with the larger conurbation of Birmingham but was not selected. Had he been considered the man for the job it is quite probable that no twentieth century ferry would have been born on the Old Passage.

Shortly after demob Enoch was visiting a site as architect when a chance conversation with a friend, Walter Watts, sowed the seed that was to change the course of his life. Watts related how during the war years he was employed as a lorry driver between Newport and Bristol and became heartily sick of the long trek around the Severn via Gloucester when a bridge or ferry down stream would have saved time and expense. Most people would probably have retorted that perhaps somebody would oblige some day and left it at that but, fresh from his experiences at Richborough, Enoch was quick to realize the potential of the estuary as a means of communication, rather than a barrier. The first job was to examine the coastline and in 1920 he crossed by Cambell's steamer to Weston-super-Mare and made his way up the coast. Battery Point at Portishead seemed a promising prospect but when the tide receded showing the extensive mud flats and inhospitable reefs it did not seem such a good idea. Another factor against this location is the width of the estuary which would have made operating costs prohibitive and likely to discourage rather than attract customers. New Passage, whilst offering a smaller distance to cross was ruled out because of the strong tide through 'The Shoots', plus the extensive mud banks and tracts of broken rock between the two shores. During the previous century the railway company had got round the problem by building long piers to deep water but these no longer existed and their replacement would have been an expensive undertaking.

Later the same year he and his wife drove to Beachley and looked over the pier. Ida was sceptical due to the broken down stonework and accumulations of silt and seaweed. Enoch's comment was, "If it's good enough for the ancients it's good enough for me!"

He approached the ninth Duke of Beaufort concerning the ferry rights on both sides of the river and on 31 July 1924 signed a lease in concert with Walter Watts and another backer, Samuel Dickinson Williams. It was agreed that a peppercorn rent would be paid for the first nine months and £100 in the fourth quarter. In addition the Duke would take a royalty on the gross tolls.

Initially nothing happened, then the imminent threat of a General Strike galvanized Enoch into action. It was obvious that with communications at a standstill his ferry would have a monopoly of trans-Severn traffic and it would be a suitable opportunity to introduce the service. He withdrew £500 of his savings and bought a vast number of railway sleepers to lay a duckboard pier at Aust. Existing facilities were sparse. A rough slope led down to a short stone pier whilst up stream a derelict wooden structure lay beneath the cliffs near the new bridge. These features are still visible today.

Olney Bros. of Barry were to provide the ferry boat and Horace Olney recalls well the sticky job they had building a 200 feet pier complete with hand-rails across the Severn mud.

The strike became a reality in May 1926 and Enoch hastened to Beachley thinking like most at the time that the deadlock would last for some months. In fact the strike only became general on 4th May and collapsed soon after on the 12th. Enoch returned to his job but Olney Bros. carried on.

Olney Bros. were based at Barry where they operated a fleet of pleasure-boats named *Silver King*, *Silver Queen*, *Silver Prince* and *Silver Princess*. *Silver Queen* was chosen for the ferry service at Beachley. She was a single-screw open motor-launch built for the company by Boon Bros. at Northam, Appledore in 1922. She was 48ft long and licensed to carry about seventy passengers. She sported a white hull and single mast for'ard. As no ferry had operated at the spot for some time a little local knowledge was desirable but found hard to obtain as a few locals objected to outsiders operating the service. In fact a Gloucester pilot, William Groves, knew the waters well and was a considerable help.

Much time was spent handing out leaflets to picnickers and passers-by to try and drum up business. Buses of the Bristol Tramways met the ferry which ran at hourly intervals.

An official opening took place on 6 July 1926 and was featured in the national press. Guests of honour were the Lord Mayor of Bristol, Alderman Frank More, the Lady Mayoress and the Reverend Canon T.J. Bowen, Lord Mayor's Chaplain. The *Silver Queen* was suitably decked out with bunting and a large assembly of people gathered to watch the opening ceremony and cross on the new ferry.

An announcement headed, 'August 1927' declared, 'A preliminary Service across the Severn by Swift Motor Craft carrying Passengers, Cycles, Motor Cycles and Side-cars — but NOT Motor Cars YET'. To assist the carriage of heavy and unwieldly machines Hurd and Henderson, boat-builders of Chepstow, attached a hand operated derrick to the main mast. This was quite adequate for the purpose for which it was intended but soon after the official opening Enoch decided to take his car, a Gwynne 8, across as an experiment. Considerable effort was involved due to the great weight and on arrival at Aust the car was discharged over the side on to the beach. Horace Olney can only recall two cars ever being carried as they only just fitted on to the narrow pier at Aust. These were the first vehicles to cross the water but only a few more years were to elapse before Enoch was to realize his ambition of a regular car-ferry.

The timetable declared an hourly service between 9 a.m. and 8.30 p.m., and fares for passengers one shilling, bicycles one shilling, motor cycles one shilling and sixpence, motor cycles and side-cars two shillings and sixpence, and runabouts four shillings, subject to the elements and other sources of inconvenience! In practice services terminated at dusk.

The ferry service operated all the year apart from Christmas Day but did very little business after the Summer Licence of Motor Licences ended as very few motor cyclists renewed their licence from October.

During the second winter the wooden pier at Aust was destroyed by bad weather but insurance cover enabled them to salvage what was left and rebuild the structure. Unfortunately it was completely destroyed in another storm and the service petered out in October 1928.

Horace Olney returned to Barry and continued to operate his pleasure-boat service until war broke out and his vessels were commandeered. Prior to this the *Silver Queen* was sold to a new owner at Lowestoft and sailed there in a voyage lasting three weeks across the country via Gloucester piloted by a Mr D. Alexander. The *Silver King* became a firefloat at Newport.

Olney Bros. had an option to run the ferry themselves but they did not exercise it and the rights reverted to Enoch

Williams. Prior to this a shareholder Mr Kewer-Williams realized that to operate a car-ferry it was obvious that a much bigger company was required to provide a suitable level of financial backing. Despite the fact that capital was a little sparse in the twenties he had great faith in the ferry and to try and generate interest registered a new company, 'The Severn (Beachley-Aust) Ferry Limited' with a capital of £60,000. An advertisement appeared in the *South Wales Argus* announcing the firm's intentions of transporting vehicles in an average of twelve minutes between new pier works, plans for which had been approved by the Board of Trade. Motor-ferries were to be provided capable of carrying twenty-four ordinary cars, or eight lorries, buses or motor-coaches.

The company had acquired the lease of Ferry Rights across the Severn from Portishead in the south to Lydney in the north until 1966. A subscription list was opened but nothing came of the venture due to lack of support.

CHAPTER FIVE

Success

A chance visit to a North Somerset quarry in connection with his employment as an architect led Enoch to a lifelong association with the Beauchamp family. They expressed an interest in his plans for a ferry and became shareholders in a new company registered on 11 February 1931. Named the Old Passage Severn Ferry Co. Ltd., capital was to be £3,000 in £1 shares. Objects of the new company were to 'acquire an underlease of the ferry rights over the River Severn from Beachley to Aust, together with the piers used therewith, and to carry on the business of ferry proprietors and proprietors of piers, jetties, landing stages, wharves and docks, boat, barge and steam tug owners.' The Directors were R.B. Beauchamp, Newberry House, Nr. Frome, G.W.B. and R.S.B. Beauchamp of Stratton House, Stratton-on-the Fosse; D.W.B. Beauchamp of Lipyeate House, Holcombe; E. Williams, 1 Beechdale Road, Newport. Director's qualification was £300 shares. Remuneration of E. Williams was £100 p.a. with the other directors taking £250 p.a. between them.

Events moved rapidly and the keel of the first vessel was laid the following month. A favourite saying of Enoch's was an alleged quote from Shakespeare, 'I speak four languages you know, there's English, Welsh, French and seaman's language'. By this time he was becoming quite proficient at the latter and had accumulated a few ideas as to what a Severn ferry-boat should look like. His wife was a willing source of inspiration and the next bit of my story is best told in her own words.

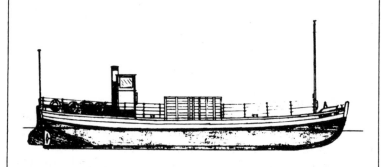

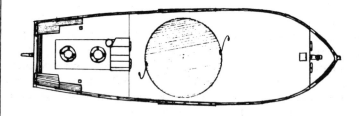

PRINCESS IDA

LENGTH 40'   BREADTH 20'

BUILT 1931 BY HURD BROS & HENDERSON, CHEPSTOW

HULL DIMENSIONS TAKEN FROM BUILDERS HALF-MODEL. UPPER WORKS AS SHE APPEARED LATER WHEEL-HOUSE ENCLOSED AND MAST ERECTED FOREWARD. NOTE ROPE-HANDLES ON TURNTABLE

'He called the new craft the *Princess Ida*, combining a tribute to me with his love for Gilbert and Sullivan. It seemed to me tragic that a space 60ft by 20ft should hold only eight cars. On that one fateful night I couldn't sleep. We had made cardboard models of the deck and a score of cars and as I tossed and turned my mind sought a method of packing them aboard. The clock struck six, and, exhausted, I fell asleep.

'In my dream, time slipped back to 1897. My grandfather the late Alderman Andrew Thomas, was conducting me around the Midland station at Bath Green Park where he was an engine driver and he took me at last to see one of the enormous engines revolving on the turn-table. I awoke in a flurry of excitement and shook my peacefully sleeping man awake with the shriek, I've got it! A turn-table!'

The firm of Hurd and Henderson contracted to build *Princess Ida* in a corner of Fairfield's Shipyard at Chepstow. She was built entirely of wood, the stem-post being selected from a suitable oak tree in Sedbury Park. The rest of the timber came from a Cardiff importer. Planking was said to be double diagonal which gave her hull tremendous strength but also meant there was plenty of 'give' so that when she grounded she did not open her seams and end her days on the bottom. A photograph of the vessel seems to contradict this and show her to be carvel built i.e. edge to edge. The hull was virtually flat-bottomed and of very shallow draught to enable her to reach the piers at most states of the tide. She only drew one foot eight inches forward and about three feet aft. A Norwegian 90 h.p. Elwe diesel engine powered a single screw. Total cost was to be £1,800.

As work progressed Enoch made the biggest decision of his working life and gave up his successful career as an architect for that of ferry-boat operator.

For £100 the company bought a large passenger launch the *May Queen* which Fairfield's at Chepstow had previously operated as a runabout. The next task was to find a skipper. This was easier said than done. In desperation Enoch tried to talk William Groves into taking the job. Bill already combined a successful sand and gravel business with that of river pilot and pleasure-boat operator so to sever his interests he requested three months to tidy up these affairs. As an alternative he suggested his brother Geoff be the first skipper. Geoff had just returned from Australia and was due to start work under John Watts of Lydney as a fitter for the future Red and White Omnibus Co. Enoch would have none of that; he wanted Geoff to sign a contract on the spot but the latter had only just got married and felt that his wife ought to have some say in the matter. Again, he had promised to start for Red and White and he did not want to make any hasty decisions. With typical impetuousity Enoch contacted John Watts and by the next day it was arranged that Geoff Groves would start on the ferry at three pounds five shillings per week and if things didn't work out his job as a fitter would be held open for three months. The brothers Bert. and Geof. Blatchford, sons of the Beachley lighthouse keeper were taken on as crew.

Services commenced on Monday 18 May 1931 with a similar fare structure to that of the *Silver Queen*. Passengers were sparse and the necessary money even thinner on the ground, consequently wages were a trifle irregular during the first few weeks. Within a short while permission was granted for the carriage of motor bikes and cycles and business grew.

July came with the Inaugural Luncheon fixed for the 30th at the Waverley Tea Gardens, Beachley. Guests had been invited but the *Ida* was still on the stocks. After feverish activity she was launched with a couple of days to spare by Mrs Williams. On the great day Alderman A.J. Proctor and a large assembly of guests and well-wishers gathered on Beachley and Aust piers to see the new boat. Geoff Groves went to the Fairfield Yard to collect the *Princess Ida* confident that she would be ready for service. Quite a shock awaited him for no crew had been taken on apart from himself as skipper at an increased wage of four pounds five shillings per week. Bob Jones was working as a shipwright for Hurd and Henderson at the time and he with some others formed a scratch crew.

Under way at last a frantic search was made for buckets and mops to make her more presentable but all in vain. On arrival at Beachley Geoff nipped ashore and met Enoch at the water's edge where he promptly informed him that the whole event would have to be called off! Enoch blanched. It was out of the question. How could he call it off? Geoff pointed out that no river trials had been made to test out the reliability of the engine, and more to the point, no Board of Trade Inspector would pass her as no fire equipment or life-saving gear was on board. Casting a quick eye over the crowd Enoch said, "I don't see any inspector. You don't intend sinking or setting fire to her do you, so what are you worried about? I accept all responsibility." With that the ceremony proceeded.

Enoch's Singer car was loaded aboard across some temporary planks as the ramps had yet to be fitted. Acclaimed as the first motor-vehicle across the ferry this was not stricly true (notwithstanding the 1926 crossings) as a short while before, Geoff Groves had been at Beachley in the *May Queen* when a frantic businessman arrived in his car and said he must get to Bristol as soon as possible as he stood to lose a lot of money. He was promptly informed that cars could not be carried and anyway they had no means to do so. The man retorted that in India he would summon a boy and for an anna he would take him across any river. Whether he expected Geoff to do likewise he did not say. The upshot was that one of the Blatchford boys ran to his father's house and obtained some timber to straddle the boat. An onlooker was engaged for the trip and after securing her across the vessel they crossed uneventfully to Aust. In return seventeen shillings and sixpence was paid out for their trouble, a lot of money in those days. Ten shillings went in the kitty and half a crown each to Geoff, the boy and the temporary help.

Enoch on hearing of the happening swore Geoff to secrecy of an event known today to only a few.

Anyway, to return to our story the official party boarded the ferry and surrounded the car and wheelhouse. The journey across to Aust commenced and all went well until the temporary engineer called up the voice-pipe for permission to stop the engine. This granted, the still boat drifted on the tide. Enoch became concerned and asked what was wrong. On investigation a worried crewman appeared holding a broken fuel pipe. Crisis! With the aid of some old cloth and some paint and putty a temporary seal was made and an attempt made to start the engine. This was easier said than done. Ignition was by a cartridge which was first heated with a match and when judged hot placed in the single cylinder head. The engine was then turned by hand to fire. All this required a certain amount of practice which nobody had received, thus the first attempt was a failure. Not so on deck. The misfiring produced a cloud of black smuts which showered Geoff's beautiful white hat and new suit to say nothing of the fine clothes of the guests. Still, they were under way.

As they approached the opposite shore a crewman was stationed at 'front and back' as Enoch would say, to moor the boat to the pier. The first cast was tied securely but promptly snapped when the *Ida* carried straight on! No telegraph was fitted between bridge and engine-room making co-ordination of docking and engine revs something of a knotty problem. Bob Jones acted as an intermediary but this didn't help appreciably since the vessel was found to be incapable of reverse. Subsequently 20(?) tons of concrete ballast was inserted to give the screw a grip on the water but this didn't help their predicament. The *Ida* churned ahead and stuck fast alongside Aust pier. Enoch was furious and another heated exchange took place with his new skipper. Geoff's solution was simple, "Give me four hours and I'll get her off. You've got the Boars Head and the New Passage at hand, take your guests there until we're back in business." This of course was the only answer. Mercifully none of this appeared in the local press which I think says something for the consideration of people's feelings in an age now passed.

Princess Ida's introduction meant a new fare structure for 'runabouts' with motor cars under 8 h.p. being carried for five shillings single and those over for six shillings. A concession for the former was six tickets for one pound four shillings and six tickets for one pound ten shillings for the latter. A considerable saving for regulars. Later, on 1 May 1933 the charges were reduced to four shillings and five shillings respectively. About this time concession tickets were abolished as some passengers abused the privilege by retaining tickets and obtaining free rides.

One journalist noted that it was cheaper to drive by way of Gloucester than across the ferry but few preferred the long journey for the sake of a few shillings extra expense.

To begin with the wheelhouse was simply an open box exposed to the elements with a reedy black exhaust pipe projecting into the air behind it. Within a short while an enclosed wheelhouse was constructed and the exhaust given a protective covering, thus giving it more the appearance of a respectable funnel.

The simple funnel marking initially adopted by the company was a broad white band on a black field. A tall flag-mast projected from the stern rail and later, following Board of Trade scrutiny, a further mast with a navigation light was attached in line with the bow railings. Her hull was painted a distinctive white all over with her name at bows and stern. As far as I can trace she was never placed on Lloyds Register of Shipping and never carried any port of registry, which would have been Newport.

The new boat could carry four large and six small cars at one crossing but as Percy Palmer informed me, the situation in the winter months was sometimes disastrous for whereas in the summer they suffered from lack of capacity at peak holiday periods, on some winter days they had little traffic at all. On one particular day a paltry seven cars crossed the water.

Passengers were plentiful and seats were provided at the stern for their use. Bert Blatchford succeeded Geoff Groves on the *May Queen* which continued to be used when only passengers turned up for the ferry. Her service came to an abrupt end in January 1936 when a terrific storm tore her loose from Beachley Pier and she hasn't been seen since.

Bob Jones, as previously stated was one of the *ad hoc* crew on the first day, and as orders in the yard were thin at the time he gave up his job to become mate on the new boat. Later Percy Palmer was to join as deck-hand under different circumstances. He was a product of the Reardon Smith National College at Cardiff and spent five years at sea until a severe bout of bronchitis laid him up at his home in Chepstow. His mother thought a spell of work on the ferry would aid his recovery before going deep water again, not realizing that he would become hooked on his convalescent employment and not leave until thirty-one years later when the ferry closed.

Early in her service the *Ida* had the misfortune to strand on Beachley Pier and suffer bottom damage; particularly to the keel. Davis's dry-dock at Saul fitted sister keelsons to avoid further damage in the event of another accident. Shortly after her return to service skipper and owner fell out once again.

The *Ida* had got well under way for Aust with two cars aboard when Enoch with his business mind noticed some further customers at Beachley Pier and ordered Geoff Groves to turn around and pick them up. As any seaman knows the skipper is in command on the boat and any decisions on her movement lie with him. After a ding-dong exchange Geoff returned to Beachley knowing that little water would now lie near the pier. His fears proved well founded for on arrival the boat stuck fast on the mud, the end result being that nobody crossed the river. Not unnaturally the two car owners already aboard were a trifle annoyed and had to be suitably compensated at heavy cost later.

Geoff left the company and was engaged for some time in an advisory capacity on preparing the Severn Bridge Bill of 1935/36, being the proud possessor of testimonials for services rendered from the government agencies involved. Bob Jones succeeded him as skipper. I must hasten to add that despite their differences both parties remained the best of friends.

The Great Western Railway Company had inaugurated a car transporter service on 7 April 1909 between Pilning and Severn Tunnel Junction via the Severn Tunnel. Vehicles were carried on flat trucks attached behind passenger trains passing through, this service operating until the opening of the Severn Bridge. At no time does this rival arrangement ever seem to have affected the ferry service or vice versa.

The job of maintaining the *Ida* and keeping some continuity of service with only one boat must have been quite a problem but to effect running repairs a grid was constructed on the up stream side of Beachley Pier close to the shore. At this time Alec Gardiner ran a small boatyard by the mouth of Lydney harbour and the *Ida* was sent there for annual overhauls, which for obvious reasons took place in winter. From time to time she had her rubbing strakes renewed at Saul and on one occasion had a new turn-table installed in her.

Neither shore provided a sheltered anchorage when the boat was not in use and at the end of the day she was moored in the Wye down stream of Chepstow Railway Bridge.

Despite the low winter figures 26,070 passengers and 5,837 cars were carried in 1932, the first year of profitable operation. The number of users proved conclusively that the Welsh Wizard's ferry was a success.

CHAPTER SIX

Expansion

Within a couple of years of commencing operations it became obvious that to cope with the increasing trade their whole operation would have to be upgraded and increasingly become an essential part of the national communications system. If this step was not taken trade would exceed capacity, the public would become disenchanted with the delays involved and business would decline, or at worst might stimulate a rival service.

The only answer was to expand. A visit was made to Antwerp to inspect a pair of second-hand ferry-boats but the decision was taken to build new and incorporate their own ideas based on operational experience on the Severn.

A contract was placed with Woodward and Scarr of Beverley, Yorks to build two new vessels that would provide a continuous service between Beachley and Aust. They were to be twin engined driving twin screws, as a great failing of the *Princess Ida* was her lack of manoeuvrability in the strong river currents when approaching or leaving a pier. Crossley engines of 220 h.p. were to be installed in an all steel hull. When seen at low tide sitting on the mud both vessels had something of an appearance of a flattened pudding basin with a large rim. This was because the boats would be expected to spend much of their life aground on the gently shelving shore-line and the absence of a pronounced keel would allow the boats to operate in very shallow water. Enoch had noticed that the continental boats carried a greater number of vehicles by having a deck projecting beyond the hull, suitably protected by large bulwarks. Like the *Princess Ida* a large turn-table was installed for'ard to manoeuvre vehicles into position. Adjacent ramps, like the turn-table, were to be muscle powered.

To accommodate the larger vessels and anticipated increase in traffic, considerable rebuilding took place at Beachley and Aust. The stone pier at Beachley was reinforced and on the other side a massive timber pier was constructed to connect the top, middle and lower stone piers at a cost of between £7,000 and £8,000. Creosoted twelve inch by twelve inch baulks of pitch pine were supplied by Denny Mott and Dickson at Newport, a firm still in business today. No attempt was made to dredge access channels as the river would soon have refilled any excavation. At its best the river resembles brown windsor soup, so heavy is the quantity of sediment in suspension.

Towards the end of June 1934 the new pier was nearly finished but delivery of the first vessel was delayed. Construction of Aust Pier had proceeded without incident until two lorries delivering stone from Cromhall got stuck at the end of the slipway. The ignition system of the first had been soaked by spray and the driver of the second lorry went to help. His lorry suffered the same fate. A rising tide soon enveloped both vehicles which gradually slid overboard into the river, one overturning. Both were extricated with difficulty.

Whilst all this activity was in progress *Princess Ida* soldiered on, but on Tuesday 27 February 1934 she suffered another stranding. Percy Palmer recalled it well. They had embarked two cars at Aust amidst tremendous winds and a rough sea. As the boat went astern to clear the pier a blast caught her and swept her sideways on to the submerged slipway. The tide receded leaving her high and dry but she was refloated at 3.30 p.m. the same day without apparent damage. Just in case of damage she was sent to Charles Hill's at Bristol for dry-dock inspection.

Despite such diversions she seems to have been a reliable vessel for during the August Bank Holiday week she carried over 1,000 cars and 4,000 passengers. The queues must have been a foretaste of things to come. Since starting in 1931 she had carried about 60,000 cars.

Later that year Beverley saw the launching of the first new ferry. Miss Woodward performed the launching ceremony naming her *Severn Queen*, before she slid sideways into the river with a mighty splash. No publicity was given to the event but her delivery and first trial trip on Monday 26th November received excellent coverage.

She had rather a sombre appearance being painted black all over, and only relieved by her name painted in large letters on the bows. Her flush deck had a small wheelhouse towards the stern permitting cars to be parked either side of it. To brighten her the bulwarks were painted white soon after with the name in black, this colour scheme being repeated on the later vessels. She was considerably bigger than her predecessor being 75 feet long and 30 feet beam; drawing 4 feet 6 inches aft and 2 feet 6 inches for'ard. She weighed 90 tons and could carry a load of 25 tons. Delivery from Hull had taken eight days.

On board for the first crossing was Enoch Williams, the Managing Director and Directors Ralph Beauchamp, Gilbert Beauchamp, Ross Beauchamp and Dudley Beauchamp. Mr E. Woodward, Director of the building company and Mr W.H. Jarret the designer showed commendable faith in their product by being aboard with them, the actual crossing skippered by Bob Jones taking eight minutes.

Mr Jarrett expressed complete satisfaction with the performance of the *Severn Queen* after she had done two trips on the service. Later in discussion about their design he commented on the similarity in type to ferries operating on American Rivers. They were technically known as the scaw type, with shallow draft, good beam and plenty of power.

About this time William Groves decided to join the company as skipper of the *Severn King*, becoming a personal friend in the years to come, as he was to many of the regulars. His 'Players medium navy cut' beard was most distinctive and a welcoming sight on the bridge.

Prince Paul of Greece became the first member of any Royal Family to use the new ferry when he crossed to stay with Lord Tredegar at Tredegar Park in April 1935.

Princess Ida continued to share the service but went into reserve with the arrival of the *Severn King*. Launched in June she was introduced without ceremony but an advertisement dated 3 August 1935 announced that two new ferries were now in service with accommodation for thirty-seven cars on a half-hourly service. Her hull was basically the same as her twin but there the similarity ended. To allow more space for vehicles a bridge deck supported by small wings gave a completely unobstructed deck fore and aft. A little protection from the weather was afforded to pedestrians by this structure but seating was only provided in the open adjacent to the wheel-house. The additional weight gave her a very tail end heavy appearance which was never rectified despite the additional weight of concrete ballast amidships and in the forward compartments giving her a draught of 5 feet 6 inches aft and 3 feet forward. Surprisingly her overall tonnage was less than that of her predecessor.

From the beginning both vessels went to Charles Hill at Bristol for annual overhaul at their Albion Dockyard, the lock at Lydney being too narrow to accommodate them. Each vessel was sent in rotation during the winter months when traffic would be least affected by the reduction in capacity.

Wear and tear on machinery was considerable with a number of engine renewals over the years culminating in a final change to Leyland diesels in the late fifties in line with their new vessel to supplement the existing fleet. Service speed averaged eight to nine knots but this was considered of less importance to that of good manoeuvrability from twin screws and a reserve of power for the unexpected situations that could and did arise in berthing in the fickle river currents.

When the water was too low for service the vessels normally moored in the Wye, but late in 1935 Gloucester Harbour Trustees gave permission for Northwick Buoy to be used as a mooring, this being situated down stream of Aust off the Gloucestershire shore. Its use was subject to other vessels, presumably laden cargo boats, having priority. During the war years grain elevators were towed to the buoy from Sharpness to discharge large ocean freighters, the *clank-clank* of the elevator far into the night becoming a familiar sound across the near-by lonely marshes.

As in the previous century the ferry has always operated with the threat of a bridge taking over its role. This story has been well told elsewhere but by the mid-thirties construction seemed imminent. Unfortunately international affairs began to take a hand as Germany grew in power and plans came to a sudden halt. For years everyone had accepted the economic necessity of a bridge between the industrial areas of South Wales and the consumer markets of the south of England. Not without protest the then Minister of Transport, Hore-Belisha, announced to the Commons on the evening of 6 November 1935 that because of the importance of the National Defence Programme plans for a Severn Bridge had to be shelved.

With two new boats in service the ferry could now expect a monopoly of the traffic and experienced a heavy increase in use following the cancellation of the bridge project. Heavy gales early the following year caused extensive damage at Beachley, lifting the huge stone facing blocks away from the edge of the pier and scattering them about like toy bricks.

Somewhere around this period one of the skippers nearly lost his life. The day's work finished and one of the boats was nosing up to the buoy in the Wye. As deck-hand Percy Palmer was standing on the buoy detaching the dinghy ready to take the crew ashore he heard a splash. Charlie Savage had fallen in and was being carried away down stream. Quick as a flash Percy rowed after him and yanked him out almost drowned, since Charlie couldn't swim. Charlie went on to serve as a skipper to the close of the company. A similar rescue took place one Sunday afternoon at low water. On passage from Beachley to Aust Percy saw two strangers pass up stream in a dinghy. On arrival he followed them with binoculars and saw the boat hit Whirl-end sandbank and overturn. Calling for full revs he sent the boat in pursuit and plucked a father and son from the water, their only means of support being a plastic water bottle.

Business continued to gain momentum and a steady reliable service became the rule, with no particular crisis to interrupt the flow of the traffic. The ferry had become an accepted part of everyone's life but year after year the queues at Bank Holidays continued to be a source of irritation as the crowds headed for the scenic delights of the Wye Valley and Forest of Dean.

CHAPTER SEVEN

War Years

With the outbreak of hostilities in 1939 all staff in post had to stay in the employ of the company. Traffic continued to flow but the accent changed from tourist to military. By far the greater number of vehicles were American. This represented quite an attraction for the young and not so young. The phrase, 'Any gum chum?' was often heard and frequently rewarded. The pressures to give priority to particular people to cross at various times were great, especially when night approached and a queue remained. Ben Brown has vivid recollections of a military officer who insisted that he be given a place on the boat. The upshot was that the major was ordered at the point of a revolver to remain where he was. Rather an unsavoury incident for all concerned. On another occasion a gum chewing American major was given a long lecture on the Roman origins of the ferry by Enoch. As the *Queen* came alongside he drawled (shifting the plug to the opposite molar) "Same boats! Heh?"

Many bombs were dropped in the vicinity and included their quota of duds. By arrangement the ferry company carried a large quantity of defused explosives and dumped them in a deep in the river.

Heavily loaded lorries were a regular problem but on one occasion a lorry loaded with pipes started to lose its load as it attempted to mount the ramp on to the ferry. Two ammunition lorries were following close behind and the drivers went to help. Unfortunately the hand-brakes on both lorries failed to hold them and they ran into the river. Both were eventually extricated complete with their loads.

Dukws frequently used the pier as a means of entering the river when in transit but on several occasions they were swept away by the strong tide, fortunately being retrieved without loss of life. After that they were linked together and travelled across in convoy.

When air-raid warnings were received the Alway family always retreated to the room nearest the hill on the ground floor of the Old Passage House. Grandma always swore that the many feet of masonry surrounding them was safer than any air-raid shelter. It often happened that passengers in transit witnessed the war in close-up. Mrs Alway recalls as a child watching the gunning down of a German plane and seeing it crash into the sea.

Many of the staff alternated between deck-hand, engineer and office-boy depending on the traffic and other factors but Percy Palmer was fortunate to go one step further. During the early years Bob Jones was skipper of the *Severn King* but failed to turn up at 8 a.m. one morning at her Chepstow mooring. By 8.20 the crew were wondering what to do and Percy said that if Bob hadn't arrived in ten minutes he'd take her around himself. He ran her for a day and bumped the pier a few times but managed to get by. News came that Bob Jones would be out sick for a while and Percy was asked to carry on, his initiative having had its reward. During the war they all worked a six day week and his rota then became something like this; first day skipper on the *King*, second, skipper on the *Queen*, third, engineer on the *King*, fourth, engineer on the *Queen*, fifth in Aust office, sixth in Beachley office, seventh day off. Never a dull moment!

Many of the men had connections with, or possessed rights to fish the salmon on Wye and Severn. One day Percy was sculling Bill Groves and Bob Jones up towards Chepstow when the latter sighted a large fish coming towards them. Grabbing a piece of old sacking Bob successfully scooped out the fish only to lose it through a hole in the rotten material. A favourite boast of his was that he knew every rock in the river until one day whilst rowing a crew up stream he rammed one that he didn't.

A regular user prior to and during the war was Queen Mary *en route* to stay with Lord and Lady Bledisloe at their estate near by. Various versions of this tale are told but Enoch tells me that on one occasion he was standing next to Queen Mary at Aust awaiting the boat and she remarked that she had heard of the Severn Bore but never seen it. Enoch replied, "Madam, you need go no further, you're looking at him now."

One of Percy's most treasured possessions is a letter from the famous aviatrix Amy Johnson. She had run out of petrol and had no coupons to enable her to purchase more for her car. He lent her some of his but she was able to obtain sufficient fuel without using them and returned them later.

For the *Severn King* and *Queen* the war passed without mishap. The only noticeable change to them during these years was the removal of the ship's name from the hull. Even this was a later alteration as a picture taken in 1940 shows Queen Mary crossing on the *Severn King* with the name clearly legible. At one time Enoch devised his own camouflage with wavy lines painted along the hull.

Percy recalls that many famous people passed over the ferry many of whom are possibly better known to older generations. He particularly remembers Lloyd George before the war but ENSA troop entertainers and personalities such as the Western Brothers, the Two Leslies, Arthur English, Beryl Ord, Richard Dimbleby, Lord Jersey and Virginia Cherrill, Charlie Kunz, David Niven and Tessie O'Shea were recalled. Also Haile Selassie, Princess Margaret and the then Princess Elizabeth were frequent passengers.

During these years many schools were evacuated and one Bristol school was despatched to St Briavels in the Forest of Dean. A well-known Bristol cleric was a frequent visitor and became over-confident in the use of the ferry. Sitting in his Austin 10 on the turn-table on one of the boats he drove off before it had stopped with disastrous results. He clouted the wing of a stationary car whose irate driver quickly appeared and muttered, "Jesus Christ!" when he saw the damage. The Reverend turned to Percy Palmer without blinking and said, "I think he said that for the benefit of my collar."

On a later occasion Ben Brown was absent-mindedly leaning on the wing of a car whilst in transit and got a broken nose for his impudence.

A well-remembered character was a travelling salesman for Parkinson's Butterscotch called Roberts. He was singularly remarkable for his enormous size and reputation that when visiting his customers he would sit outside a shop and beep the horn until the owner appeared to make his order. He never left the car if he could help it and nearly always slept on the voyage despite its short duration. On one visit he arrived at 1.30 p.m. to find no boat in sight so settled down for a snooze. At 6 p.m. the call of nature forced him to dismount and he then saw a notice pinned to the office door saying the service was suspended. You will recall it's 55 miles to Chepstow via Gloucester.

A small gun emplacement was built on Beachley pier more for morale than military significance but I'm told a trigger-happy cleric eagerly manned the post whenever the air-raid sounded and used every low flying intruder as an excuse for target practice. After one particular episode the dismantled weapon was brought into Beachley pier office where Enoch was making up the books. It was soon discovered that, 'One remained up the spout' for on being dropped on the floor it discharged with a loud report into the table leg. The exchange of words that followed is not recorded.

CHAPTER EIGHT

Call-Up

About 1941 H.M.S. *Vernon* at Portsmouth was carrying out trials on mines and required a suitable vessel to retrieve experimental weapons from the sea and shore.

Captain E.J. Wide the Piermaster at Birnbeck was sent to Beachley to inspect *Princess Ida* which had been brought from her berth in the Wye to the grid on the north side of the Beachley slip. The requirement was that she should have a low magnetism as she was to be used in testing magnetic mines in particular. As she was built entirely of wood she was thought suitable for use and was requisitioned by the Admiralty.

As a boy John Alway often visited the pier and remembered the occasion well. His mother took him down to see the strange boat which had been laid up for some time in the Wye. To John she seemed large and white with many men in uniform looking her over.

Shortly after, Charlie Savage skippered her to Cardiff with Jim Hawker as engineer and Percy Palmer as deck-hand. None of them ever saw her again; the common belief being that she was to be used for towing targets.

After overhaul she was reportedly used for experimental torpedo work at Milford Haven and then sent across to H.M.S. *Birnbeck*, the old pier at Weston-super-Mare. Painted service grey she bore no identification and was simply known as the *Birnbeck*. There seems to be no record of her being commissioned as H.M.S. *Birnbeck* but she acquired the name by usage.

When not in use she was anchored in the Axe Estuary off Uphill. She would then go round to Birnbeck skippered by a petty officer with a leading stoker acting as engineer. Extra crew would be taken on as required. Having arrived at the pier the mines would be winched by derrick on to the deck and the same in reverse as required. A hand winch was attached to the foremast for retrieving the mines from the beach. The only other alteration to the original vessel was the luxury of electric lighting. Two locals, Jack Smith and Bob Crowe carried out routine maintenance on the engine but for bigger jobs she went to P.K. Harris and Sons' yard at Appledore where a dry-dock was available. Most of her time was spent in Sand Bay but as the war progressed trials were moved to the more secluded Woodspring Bay and the Langford Grounds. *Birnbeck* often spent time anchored there to save returning to the Axe.

She normally carried eight or nine 3,000 lb mines but it was felt that the craft would benefit from some strengthening of the deck supports. She was therefore sent down to Appledore where steel struts were installed and returned to her berth in the Axe. The next day the skipper was horrified to see a distorted deck and daylight showing between it and the hull. It appeared that as the wooden hull settled on the mud and the tide receded the natural give in her timbers was interrupted by the steel strutting and something had to move. The deck sprung amidships and the *Birnbeck* had to be returned to Appledore for complete strengthening. On another occasion *Birnbeck* sprang a leak and had to be beached off Brean Down, being pumped out and returned to the Axe the next day.

The most spectacular incident was when an over zealous skipper brought her up the Axe too soon on the highest tide of the year, anchored her and went home. Next morning a rather shocked cox'n telephoned Captain Wide and said that the *Birnbeck* was high and dry. The Axe Estuary is banked by extensive saltings which are grazed for most of the year. When they arrived to see the accident the *Birnbeck* was sitting on the grass surrounded by cows! Urgent action was required to get her off and a tug was sent from Cardiff to tow her clear on the next tide. Unfortunately the tug went to Burnham instead and the opportunity was lost. The ballast had been removed but the tide failed to even reach her.

Fortunately for all concerned Bob Crowe had a brainwave and as a member of the Auxiliary Fire Service borrowed the Dennis fire engine from Weston and blasted away the mud from around and beneath the hull. She floated off about a week later but had the floating capability of a collander, requiring a fire pump running continually to keep her from sinking.

27 March 1943 saw *Birnbeck* grounded near the Howe Rock on Brean Down. Fears were expressed for her crew of four as the strong west wind looked likely to drive the vessel on to the anti-invasion defences. The lifeboat *Fifi and Charles* was launched across the bay but when she arrived the vessel had refloated on the incoming tide, the crew asking to be escorted to her moorings in the river Axe.

Following the war she was laid up in Castle Pill, Milford Haven and gradually fell apart. An ignominious end after a short but busy life.

CHAPTER NINE

The Newnham Episode

With the demise of the Severn Bridge project Enoch's fertile brain turned to the problem of alternative means of crossing the Severn for the increasingly heavy loads carried on Britain's roads. His ferry was limited in the size and weight of vehicles it would carry and there were frequent delays to commercial users to whom time meant money. A bridge had been ruled out as too expensive but it was proposed as far back as 1810 to tunnel under the river between Arlingham and Newnham. There were too many unknowns with this idea and the over and under suggestions were abandoned in favour of a surface link.

On 17 February 1939 it was publicly announced that the Old Passage Severn Ferry Co., had previously acquired the ferry rights at Newnham and intended to establish a chain-ferry across the river.

Works required were (a) an open-piled concrete pier on east bank to low water; (b) an approach road and bridge over the Passage Pill near the New Inn, Arlingham; (c) removal of rock on the west bank to form a landing and (d) laying of ferry chains across the river.

War intervened and the project was put on ice, but when peace was concluded interest revived. During the war years a man of vast imagination by the name of Ronald Marsden Hamilton evolved a unique form of floating platform designed for rapid assembly afloat in wartime conditions. Code named LILY the system never saw operational use but was put into

67

production to use in the Pacific Theatre during the advance on Japan as a floating airfield. The H-bomb put a sudden stop to plans but Hamilton realized the peacetime potential of his invention and set out to exploit it when the patent rights were returned to him. Grand ideas were mooted to construct vast floating airfields, car parks and similar projects all over the world but nothing concrete ever transpired.

Enoch Williams saw the scheme had possibilities and it was announced in the press in late 1948 that approval had been given for a crossing and the chain-ferry was abandoned in favour of a floating bridge. It was thought that for £25,000 the dreams of heavy lorries trundling across the Severn would soon become a reality.

The bridge was composed of hexagonal floats, six feet wide and thirty inches deep. These were linked together by an ingenious system of loose bolting which allowed the platform to move according to the undulations of the river. Large concrete anchorage bays were built on both sides of the river at Newnham and Arlingham.

By February 1949 hopes were expressed that the bridge would be in operation that summer but due to the severe scour of the river the anchorages wouldn't hold the floats in place. When they did hold, the cables tilted the edge of the raft at a dangerous angle. Depending on the state of the tide the bridge looped up or down river and only when the tide was at slack water did the pontoon follow a reasonably straight course. Such a set-up represented an unsatisfactory prospect for commercial use and no solution could be found. With regret the project was abandoned with a loss to the company of £20,000. Proposals were made at a later date for a structure which would withstand wind and tide but nothing came of this. A legacy of the scheme was a residue of floats which were utilized as a floating pier at St Pierre for Chepstow Yacht Club. Dubbed somewhat irreverently lily cans they were towed to the site in strings from Arlingham during 1956.

CHAPTER TEN

Peace

Services carried on as normal but disaster struck in the autumn of 1945. Tremendous gales swept the coast and carried away a one hundred foot section of Aust Pier. Initially Enoch was optimistic that services would be resumed within a short space of time but contractors could not be found to do the job and the situation looked desperate. Enoch recalled that the then Minister of War Transport, Mr Alfred Barnes had visited the ferry only a short while before and had said that if ever Enoch was in a fix he should let him know.

It worked like a charm. Men from 591 Airborne Squadron Royal Engineers were despatched from Bulford Camp to Aust and in no time at all had strengthened the remaining piers and laid a Bailey bridge across the gap capable of standing up to twenty-four tons weight. Christened Pegasus after the squadron crest the bridge was opened on November 4th by Enoch Williams taking his own car down on to the jetty.

Peace brought renewed hopes for a Severn Bridge but at the 1946 Inquiry it was stated that the ninth Duke of Beaufort had granted a licence to the ferry operators in 1927 and had renewed it for a further twenty-one years in 1945. The question of compensation must have loomed large in many minds particularly when statistics of traffic were quoted. Between May 1931 and December 1935 256,771 passengers were carried, plus 17,624 bicycles, 14,903 motor cycles, 3,015 motor-cycle combinations; 85,628 lorries and cars.

During the war 14,000 British Army and 30,000 American

69

Army vehicles were carried whilst in the first six months of 1946 155,000(?) passengers, 4,000 motor cycles, 691 motor-cycle combinations, 7,000 bicycles, 47,000 motor cars and 1,800 lorries were said to have crossed the ferry. The demise of the push-bike and the ascendance of the private car over such a small number of years is most marked. Assurances were given at the Inquiry that the ferry would continue until the bridge opened and the operators suitably compensated but these remained problems for the future.

There were lighter moments. John Alway recalls that he took the helm when only a boy much to the consternation of the passengers looking up from the deck. Bill Groves would sit at the back of the little wheel-house with only his peaked cap visible quietly smoking his pipe and keeping a watchful eye on his deputy.

Ben Brown had a favourite trick of speaking to passengers as if renewing an old friendship, or somehow invent a mutual acquaintance no matter how remote a corner of the earth the encounter was supposed to have taken place. He would frequently astonish people with his apparent knowledge of them and their affairs but like any good detective he simply built up his story from such evidence as luggage labels, accents, dress and so on, but above all his uncanny ability to size up people and understand them. The more involved he became the better he liked it and rarely came unstuck.

For many years the sailing vessel as a means of trade had virtually disappeared from the Severn Estuary apart from a few ketches and schooners that soldiered on. Among them was the *William Ashburner*, an attractive schooner frequently seen in the dock at Lydney and in the Wye. She came to grief on 9 August 1952 when she was reported adrift in the Severn, subsequently grounding on Western Point in the mouth of the Wye. The *Severn King* and *Queen* towed her off and took her to the Grain Wharf at Chepstow where she remained for some considerable time. At a later date she was in trouble again at Western Point, but this time she did not escape. Judged a danger to navigation she was blown apart with the result that only her keel and a few ribs now poke above the mud.

Moving the boats in the Wye ensured a sheltered anchorage but the tide rip was a constant difficulty. At various times all the boats broke adrift from their moorings and drifted up stream, on one occasion as far as Tintern. The spring tide can give a rise of forty feet whilst the ebb normally runs at thirteen to fourteen knots. Not unnaturally such predicaments were best forgotten but the *Severn Queen* hit the headlines in 1953 when she drifted against Chepstow Bridge and threatened to jam beneath its centre span on the rising tide. Seeing the dangerous situation from his near-by house William Groves rapidly boarded the unmanned vessel and sawed the mast off just above the deck. Freed of her obstruction the itinerant ferry swirled between the piers and was nosed into the river bank by her temporary skipper. Enoch and an engineer hastened to the scene and when the tide turned she was reversed to the arch to test her clearance. When the tide was judged to have dropped sufficiently she was turned and passed safely beneath the bridge, undamaged apart from her decapitated mast. The prospect of an Old Passage ferry floating up the Wye with Chepstow Bridge aboard was a source of nightmares on a number of occasions. January 1952 saw the fleet nearly reduced by half. In the early hours of Thursday the 24th an engine driver reported at Lydney signal box that he had seen what appeared to be a boat on fire down stream of Chepstow railway bridge. The fire brigade contacted Bill Groves with a view to getting to the fire in his launch *Firefly*. Unfortunately she was high and dry so he borrowed a fishing boat and took some firemen and a portable pump down stream. Meanwhile, a searchlight had been erected on the jetty showing the fire to be on the bridge of the *Severn King*. The Water Bailiff Mr E. Childs took out some more firemen and they soon had the blaze under control. Investigation revealed that hot cinders discharged from the funnel had landed on the wooden deck and set it alight along with some of the safety equipment. Fortunately the deck was damp after rain otherwise the boat could easily have burnt to a cinder. She returned to service the same day.

Towards the end of 1957 the *Severn King* had been sent to Charles Hill's at Bristol for the fitting of twin funnels, one each side of the bridge, replacing the single stack behind the wheel-house. Her insurers considered that an overheated exhaust may have caused the fire on the bridge deck and the removal of the bends in the exhaust system would lower the risk of a disaster. Many thought the rebuild improved her appearance. It certainly made her more distinctive.

Considering the thousands of vehicles that used the piers at Aust and Beachley it is surprising so few accidents occurred. When something did happen it was inevitable that it was spectacular and received a measure of publicity. As each tide receded pier boys swept clear the accumulations of silt and muddy water but the wet stonework still required a certain degree of caution when embarking or disembarking from the ferry. On the day in question an elderly couple were negotiating the ramp from the ferry on to Beachley pier in their Daimler Conquest car but somehow reversed in a semi-circle clean off the pier and dropped about twelve feet into the water. Fortunately the car remained upright and settled on the bottom with the usual Severn brew swirling over the bonnet. John Williams rushed down the pier and waded in, attaching a rope to the back bumper of the car. As the tide was ebbing fast the couple elected to stay put and sat Canute-like for thirty minutes with their head and shoulders above the water, only leaving when the tide had receded sufficiently to open a door. None the worse for their dip they had a warm bath and bed provided at the Ferry Hotel. The car was undamaged. The incident prompted some heated exchanges in the regional press as to the safety of the ferry and questions raised by local M.P.s requested some date for the building of a Severn Bridge but were only told that the Government had no plans for one in its road spending estimates.

The fifties and early sixties witnessed the success of Bristol Aircraft Company's *Britannia*, with the aircraft on test becoming a frequent sight within the Severn Basin. On the morning of 4 February 1954 the ferry crew watched horrified as the second prototype *Britannia, G-ALRX*, pancaked on the mud flats at Littleton-upon-Severn after an in-flight fire had started on the starboard inner engine over Ledbury. Test pilot A.J. Pegg got her down safely and the crew quickly evacuated but the aircraft, despite remaining intact, was soon claimed by the rising tide and became a total loss.

CHAPTER ELEVEN

A Royal Affair

One of Enoch's most treasured memories concerns the Queen and Duke of Edinburgh's official visit to Worcestershire and Herefordshire in April 1957. At the close of this tour they crossed the Severn for the three day event at Badminton as guests of the Duke of Beaufort.

Considerable preparations had to be made. H.M.S. *Venturer* of the Severn Division R.N.V.R. was chosen as guardship for the crossing. A 500-ton coastal minesweeper, she was and still is based at Mardyke in Bristol City Docks. Two crews and a doctor were provided on the *Severn King*, Enoch's son-in-law Dr Lyn Jones fulfilling the latter function. He had completed his naval training at H.M.S. *Royal Arthur*, Corsham when the Duke had also been there. Charles Savage was to skipper the *King* with William Groves, out of retirement for the occasion.

Wednesday April the 24th arrived and houses on both sides of the river were festooned with flags, one at Aust in particular sporting an enormous Red Ensign. About 5,000 people assembled on both banks in a biting cold wind but at 8 p.m. their patience was rewarded.

As the royal cars moved into place on the immaculate *Severn King* William Groves broke the Royal Standard from the masthead. The Duke alighted from the car and shook hands with Charles Savage, the Queen leaving later as the vessel moved away from Beachley Pier. *Venturer* dressed overall lay in mid-stream and skipper Savage took his boat

73

down the starboard side to cheers from the assembled crew. The *Severn Queen* was then passed performing the last ferry of the evening while a yellow-sailed dinghy was noted as unofficial escort. The Duke of Beaufort, Enoch and John Williams crossed with the party but first off the boat was Colonel Henn, Chief Constable of Gloucestershire. The cars were soon on their way to the cheers of the many onlookers whilst H.M.S. *Venturer* turned and slid down stream on the ebb tide. Commodore Pollinger and Commander Mc-Naughton Wainwright managed to make Avonmouth by low water but had to wait a considerable time before the flood-tide allowed them to return to their berth at Bristol.

The next meeting of the Royal couple and the ferry was to be a sadder occasion.

Recalling the day to me, John Alway described it as something of a non-event for him for when the Queen passed him at Aust and he pressed the button on his camera he found he had not wound on the film. I know the feeling.

A former Severn trow the *Alma* provided a change from the routine of ferrying in November 1958. She was built at Gloucester in 1854 and could carry 140 tons of cargo. She traded in sail to 1939 but was reduced to being towed by others as a barge thereafter. One Sunday morning she broke from her moorings at Chepstow and was seen grounded at Mathern a few days later. The *Severn King* went to retrieve her but she disappeared again, only to turn up the next day resting next to another wreck on the mud at the mouth of the Wye. Skipper Percy Palmer, Tom Lanham and John Williams boarded the holed vessel and rigged some buoys and a mast to warn shipping of the wreck. I think she was blown up soon after to clear the obstruction. Bill Groves says it was intended that she become a base for the Chepstow Sailing Club but this was not to be. Her steering wheel now adorns the fence of his garden overlooking the Wye.

CHAPTER TWELVE

A New Addition

For years there had been a general clamour for increased services at peak periods but with any profit-making concern regard had to be made to the lean times in between when idle boats were an unthinkable luxury. A happy medium had to be found but there was no doubt that another vessel was required.

A few years before, introduction of a new vessel had been considered and plans drawn up. The scheme was not proceeded with but it is interesting to examine what might have been. The vessel has a superficial resemblance to the existing *Queen* and *King* but her overall dimensions were scaled up. A larger turn-table was proposed with a modern looking flying bridge similar to the *King* but with large side cabins below an extensive bridge deck. The wheel-house was to be situated in a forward island structure with passenger accommodation behind. Twin exhausts integrated into the rear structure removed the need for a funnel. From the general arrangement I think she would have been a big success with Old Passage customers but some concern was felt for the overall hull design below the water line and her high cost. To aid manoeuvrability twin rudders were intended. The newcomer was to be of more traditional design.

Woodward and Scarr had ceased to trade before the Second World War but a near-by firm, the Yorkshire Dry-Dock Co., of Lime Street, Hull were selected to undertake the building of the vessel.

Percy Palmer was chosen to be skipper of the new ferry and

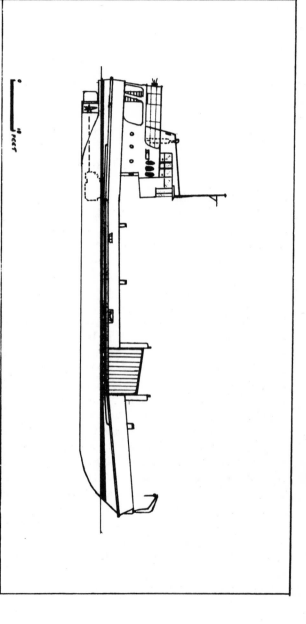

1954 PROPOSAL FOR NEW AUST - BEACHLEY FERRY

FEATURES— 18½" TURNTABLE OPP 9'9" PORT & STARBOARD RAMPS.

PASSENGER ACCOMODATION TO REAR OF WHEELHOUSE.

TWIN 150 H.P. DIESELS DRIVING TWIN PROPS. OPPOSITE TWIN RUDDERS.

TWIN EXHAUSTS AT REAR OF BRIDGE.

DIMENSIONS
LENGTH OVERALL 88'6"
BEAM OVER SPONSONS 33'0"
DEPTH MOULDED 6'9"

0 ___ 10 FEET

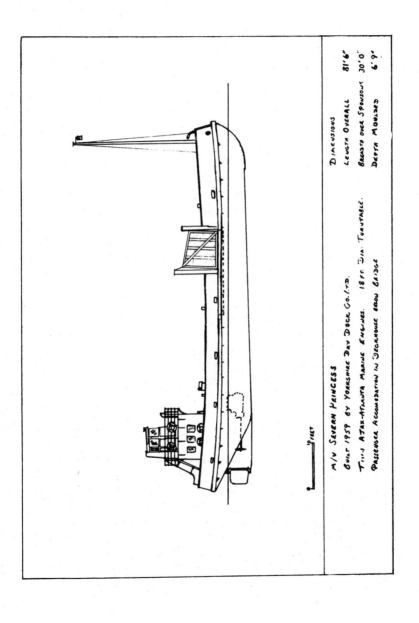

M/V SEVERN PRINCESS

BUILT 1959 BY YORKSHIRE DRY DOCK CO. LTD.

TWIN ATAX-ATLANTA MARINE ENGINES.   18FT. DIA. TURNTABLE.

PASSENGER ACCOMODATION IN DECKHOUSE BROW BRIDGE

4 FEET

DIMENSIONS

LENGTH OVERALL   81' 6"

BREADTH OVER SPONSONS   30' 0"

DEPTH MOULDED   6' 9"

made a number of trips to Hull with Enoch to inspect and advise on the construction as building proceeded. Launching took place on 23 May 1959 with Gilbert Beauchamp's daughter, Mrs Trevithick, performing the christening before the *Severn Princess* slid sideways with a mighty splash into the river. She was of similar layout to the *Severn Queen* but had limited passenger accommodation incorporated below the wheel-house. She had deck space for eighteen cars and the ramps were mechanically powered. Two Leyland engines gave a performance much improved on her sisters despite her greater size and weight. She drew about five feet aft and two feet for'ard and Percy found that she could do about fourteen to fifteen knots. Total cost was £35,000.

By the middle of June she was ready to leave and Director John Williams and brother-in-law Dr Lyn Jones signed on as seamen with the maker's crew. Percy skippered with a master mariner shipped for the trip. The journey was to be made non-stop and was expected to take five days with all crew working shifts. A caravan was tied down in front of the bridge to provide accommodation.

River trials completed the *Severn Princess* headed for the open sea. At the mouth of the Humber a ball-race in a pump failed but they decided to press on. A call for repairs was made at Weymouth before rounding Lands End and heading for the Wye. The whole journey taking between six and seven days. At Chepstow she was fitted out for service and taken round to Beachley for removal of the caravan. With the arrival of the vessel Enoch expected to be able to cope with 25,000 cars a month and increase the frequency of service from thirty to twenty minutes.

Percy remained with the *Princess* to closure, completing thirty-one years on the ferry service. One of the dirtiest jobs he did with her occurred when they were returning to Chepstow at the end of a day's service. A cow had fallen down the cliff and stood looking rather forlorn on the bank. To get at her they had to cross the extensive mud flat exposed by low water. Eventually they managed with ropes and human muscle to return her to the top but not before they were all thoroughly plastered in mud and other noisome matter of questionable source!

CHAPTER THIRTEEN

The Beginning of the End

Approval for a Severn Bridge was now given but fears were again expressed that the ferry would cease to function. The main difficulty arose over the close proximity of construction work to Beachley pier and the silting up of the berths by the building up stream of a protective screen to slow the river's force. Services were continued but only by using the upper side of the pier.

It seems to be an historical fact that with most large construction jobs there are the inevitable accidents with loss of human life. On the Sunday afternoon of 19 November 1961 three men working for John Howard & Co. on the bridge foundations were launching a boat when the fierce current dragged them into the river and swept them up stream.

The alarm was raised and the *Severn Princess* approaching Beachley on the last trip of the day put about and went in search. Aboard were skipper Percy Palmer, John Williams, T. Lanham engineer and Jack Bollen deck-hand. By this time dusk was falling and the chance of finding anyone alive in the freezing river was remote. One man was found opposite Littleton-upon-Severn clinging to a lifeboat. The other two were found one and a half miles up stream, one man weighing seventeen stone supporting the other. Some difficulty was experienced in getting them aboard.

Howard's own boat, the launch *Isobella* came down from Chepstow in response to the distress call and passed the *Severn Princess* on her way back to Chepstow. Rounding Beachley she drifted with the current waiting for two tankers to pass. Unfortunately she appears to have drifted into the path of both vessels and was cut in two, throwing one of the two crew into the swirling river. Weston lifeboat the *Fifi and Charles* was called out to perform what was to be her last service on the station. She picked up a raft and lifebuoy but the unfortunate man was never found.

About this time Percy had a holiday in London when he received a message to meet John and Enoch Williams at Paddington. John had heard of a motor launch hull lying at Leigh-on-Sea and was keen to inspect it. Percy was dubious but she was a good boat if they had a job in mind. Her hull was sound but she had no engines. They decided to buy her and had her shipped by low-loader lorry to the Albion Dockyard at Bristol. There Charles Hill's gave her an extensive refit and new engines and the *Mary B* was ready for service. As work progressed on the Bridge she was hired out to the contractors as a tender and towing launch skippered by Tom Lawton.

Almost a year to the day after the *Isobella* tragedy the West Country was lashed by terrific gales and heavy snow-storms. One dramatic casualty was the stranding of the naval auxiliary *Green Ranger* on the North Devon coast. She was being towed by the tug *Caswell* from Plymouth to Cardiff for refit when both were driven inshore by heavy seas and the tow parted. The crew were rescued by breeches-bouy from the cliff.

At Aust the Arctic winds made berthing difficult and freezing rain a hazard to vehicles. On the afternoon of Sunday 18 November 1962 the *Severn Queen* reversed out of Aust pier and turned to head up stream but a 'terrific gust' blew her on to the pier; Captain Ben Brown had nine cars and sixteen people in his charge all of whom had a lucky escape as the ferry sat square on the pier. At first the passengers did not realize their predicament for had the vessel sat on the edge she would have fallen off as the tide receded. However they were evacuated down a ladder placed against the hull and taken to the waiting room to await the flood tide. She refloated seven and a half hours later at 10 p.m. with the *Mary B* roped astern to assist the tow-off. As the ferry did not operate during the night hours the cars were unshipped and their owners to make the long trip to Beachley via Gloucester much to their annoyance. Their displeasure was not helped by the fact that several were short of fuel which they could not replenish because garages were closed at that hour of the night.

The *Severn Princess* did not escape unscathed that day either. Her hull caught on a steel fender at Aust which had to be hastily burned through to release her.

The mishaps did not go unnoticed. Donald Cox, M.P. for Cardiff North reckoned an inquiry was required. Mr Williams strongly rebuffed the general criticism and issued a statement to the press as follows:

'Three out of the five skippers have served the company for thirty-one, thirty and twenty-eight years respectively, the other two have been with us for more than ten years. It may interest Mr Cox to know that the first three have operated more than three hundred thousand crossings since the inauguration of the ferry service in August 1931.'

Mr Charles Laughlin M.P. for West Gloucestershire asked Ernest Marples, Minister of Transport to look into the mishaps. In a written reply the Minister said he had investigated the affair and declared, "I am satisfied that no blame attaches to the master."

There the matter rested.

Two years later an appeal by the Company against a revised rating of shore facilities gives a fair idea of the economics of running a ferry. The following figures were cited in the local press. Both Beachley and Aust had been uprated to £5,500 each, but as was pointed out if the ferry was withdrawn the buildings and facilities only had a nominal value. The assessment was reduced to £1,250 in each case. Rent in 1961 of £4,698 was paid to the Duke of Beaufort, the lease having been renewed in 1945 at £100 p.a. plus five per cent of tolls. Gross receipts for 1962 were £100,000, the profit said to be £80,000, a far cry from the years of imbalance in the late twenties.

It was common practice for road tankers to refuel the boats from the pier but sometimes mishaps occurred. One worrying day a fully loaded tanker broke through the wooden pier and stuck fast. The incoming tide threatened to engulf it and the fuel was discharged into the sea allowing the lorry to float. She was tied fast and on the ebb tide a ferry boat helped the lorry on to the pier. Unfortunately it straddled the edge and badly bent its back, giving it a camel-like appearance.

CHAPTER FOURTEEN

The End of the Road

The opening of the Severn Bridge was a momentous occasion for road users both local and national, thrusting into the background the significance of the ferry it replaced. It is something of an enigma that the vast traffic of the ferry-company had been one of the persuading factors leading to the construction of the bridge. Enoch Williams had always accepted this fact but it did not make the day of closure any happier for him.

From the annual overhauls at Charles Hill's dockyard a friendship sprang up between Alan W. Peck and Enoch Williams which is best measured by a poem composed by the former in later years as follows:

LOOK YOU!

This is a tale of a Welshman bold,
Nimble of mind, with a heart of gold
Who after the German war he fought
Was looking for outlets when he thought
As he stood by the Severn's muddy shore
Indeed! Look You! it's surely a bore
To motor so many miles and go
By Gloucester and back, he thought, and so
Why not a ferry from here to there
To carry their motors — could he dare?

Experts of course scoffed at his scheme
Said, "It's impossible, only a dream,
For the tides are great that so fiercely flow
And mud and the raging winds that blow
Would smash and shatter the pieces like trash
And ships and piers would surely crash."
He sized it up, then he went ahead,
That's years ago, now see where it's led
He owns three ships with royal names,
A thriving business and rightly claims
With the bridge being built up by the nation
He has justly earned his compensation.
Now we who always repair his ships
Have enjoyed his company (also his quips
Which burgeon forth when settling the score
Which often took many a month and more!) and
Are sending herewith the final one
For the ferry service is over and done.
May Enoch Williams and his son John
Bask in the sun as they journey on.

Compensation of £90,000 was granted to the Company but when one man has spent his whole life labouring on his first — or shall I say second? — love, money doesn't satisfy every human need.

The events of Thursday 8 September 1966 have been well recorded elsewhere but it was to be a grand finale for the ferry. Enoch was one of the official guests introduced to the Queen and later, after the final crossing on the flag bedecked *Severn Princess* he was still able to joke that "After forty years of ferrying and fifty years of married life a chap needs a rest."

Later the same day at Beachley Percy Palmer had the final word when making a presentation to Mr Williams.

"Two hours ago we made the very last trip with a ferry boat for carrying vehicles and now we can say the ferry is history. Even this hotel we are in is renamed the 'Old Ferry Hotel' from the Ferry Hotel. The History Book of Chepstow makes very interesting reading and you, Mr Williams, can be proud of adding another chapter to that book and I for one am particularly proud to have helped, in some small way. We have

spent our thirty-one years together; perhaps we have not always seen eye to eye on various problems but a good argument really hurts no one providing you remain good friends afterwards, which I think we will be. During the thirty-one years you and I have been through some smooth and some rough waters but I think we can say there is a lot we wish to remember and little we want to forget."

A tribute must be paid to all who worked on the ferry, a hard life — a man's life, but often salted with humour. Anyone who works afloat will tell you that the sea has a living soul and the Severn is no exception. Her fickleness provided a world of contrasts. On still, calm mornings the mirror-like surface reflected the flash of Dunlin, seeking the ebb tide feeding grounds. At other times the storm-tossed brown surf crashing on St Tecla's Island presented a foreboding sight. The seasons added their own variables with the dark and dismal short winter days, often with driving rain and sleet contrasting with the long balmy days of summer coping with long queues of vehicles and people, whilst daylight lasted.

Then there were the mornings of thick fog when the boats dare not venture out from the Wye, watching the clock and the growing queue of cars. Enoch would trot down to the Point, and cupping his hands would shout, "It's clear at Beachley," the booming voice of a skipper would resound back through the mist. "What?"

"It's clear at Beachley — by the time you come round you'll be able to see half-way across."

An extraordinary general meeting of the Old Passage Severn Ferry Co. Ltd., was held at St Pierre Golf and Country Club, Chepstow on 7 December 1967 when the Company was voluntarily wound up.

Enoch has no regrets. As he said at the time, "You can't stop progress. I feel though that I have provided a valuable service to the public." No one will disagree.

CHAPTER FIFTEEN

Shannon Venture

At first all three vessels looked likely to find early buyers but the months slid by and they continued to swing at their moorings in the Wye. John Williams was concerned that they would obstruct navigation in the river and the old bogey of snapped moorings was never far from his mind so crews were mustered to take them to Cardiff East Dock. Percy Palmer took his *Princess*, Bill Groves the *King* and Ben Brown the *Queen*. Many of the employees of the company had become toll collectors and inspectors on the bridge so the trip provided a change from watching cars. Every week thereafter Percy went to Cardiff to look over the boats and attend to their needs.

Earlier in 1965 the decision was taken to seek other sites to commence ferry operations and thus put to good use the redundant vessels when the Severn Bridge opened. An approach was made to the Fowey-Bodinnick Ferry with an eye to scaling up operations there but without result. At the same time an approach was made to the Irish Government to test their reaction to proposals for a Shannon Ferry. They were put in contact with the Limerick Steamship Company Limited but plans for a joint venture came to naught. A similar scheme was proposed by the Council at Downpatrick for a vehicle ferry service between Strangford and Portaferry at the entrance to Strangford Lough but after inspection the Severn vessels were not considered suitable as they could not accommodate large coaches and lorries.

Following the demise of the Shannon joint venture plan,

Clare and Limerick County Councils were approached direct. The Shannon Free Airport Development Company expressed considerable enthusiasm for the project. At the same time Messrs Turner and Hickman, shipbrokers of Glasgow, made an approach to Enoch Williams to sell the boats on his behalf. Prices quoted in reply were £27,000 for the *Princess* and £15,000 each for the *King* and *Queen*. As a result the Caledonian Steam Packet Company, Argyll and Pembrokeshire County Councils showed interest but Mr Sean Hopkins representing the Irish interests on the Shannon looked the most promising prospect, as their plans were in line with the Company's own ideas for the future. He thought £20,000 a reasonable offer for the two older boats, or £30,000 for the *Princess* and one of the others. The operational costs were then investigated at length and gradually a new company named Shannon Transport Systems Ltd. crystallized, with Old Passage interests proposing to make a substantial stake in the new concern.

A site inspection by sponsors James Gorman, and Sean Hopkins; Enoch and John Williams; a consulting engineer and marine surveyor of Bard Failte; Economist Intelligence Unit and Foynes Harbour Commissioners; Co. Clare and Co. Limerick officials took place on site in March 1967. It was generally agreed that the Clare site, Turf House Ferry, appeared satisfactory but there was some division of opinion on the Foynes site, various locations in the harbour area being a potential point of access.

Despite the enthusiasm for the Shannon venture, sale of the vessels elsewhere was still being pursued. Swiss interests considered using them on the numerous lakes and likewise a suggestion for a vehicle ferry on the River Guadiana in Portugal considered. At that time converted fishing boats carried vehicles from Vila Real across to the Spanish town of Ayamonte on an *ad hoc* basis as and when required but the bulk of their custom was supplied by a considerable pedestrian traffic. Existing operators had a monopoly and expressed interest in the Severn Ferries but did not see the necessity of buying them. The high cost of delivery proved to be an additional stumbling block. All these ventures came to naught.

Meanwhile back at home the usual red tape and endless correspondence dragged on over the Shannon project and prospects for Severn bottoms on Irish waters grew slightly dim. The brokers were advised to renew their efforts to sell elsewhere. This stimulus prompted the Irish company to express the hope that they would be in a position to buy all three vessels.

Once again outside interests requested details of the ferry-boats, this time from Malta and Pembrokeshire County Council. Again nothing materialized. By the middle of 1967 draft contracts were being prepared and it was now proposed to sell the *Princess* for £15,000 and the *King* and *Queen* for £7,599 each to the Irish Company. By the end of the year £1,000 was paid by the two sponsors and arrangements were made to transfer all three boats to Charles Hill's at Bristol for survey and repair prior to transfer to Ireland. Unfortunately for all concerned the estimates for repair and delivery far exceeded anyone's expectations, the cost in respect of the *King* and *Queen* being £1,000 in excess of their purchase price! Both vendor and purchaser immediately met when the decision was taken to rescind the agreements in respect of the *King* and *Queen* and lower the purchase price of the *Princess* to £12,000 in view of her expected £3,000 plus overhaul bill.

The *King* was soon sold elsewhere, as detailed in the next chapter, with the *Princess* ready for delivery by March 1968 but things still seemed to be going wrong.

A group of businessmen tried to persuade the Irish company to change their plans and abandon the Foynes-route in preference to a new link between Talbert and Killimer about ten miles down stream on the Shannon Estuary. Unfortunately as it turned out their arguments in favour of the new route did not sway the promoters away from Foynes and a rival organization blossomed forth. Both concerns applied for government grants for terminal facilities and the whole exercise lost momentum. Rivalry was economic suicide and the Foynes backers suspended development, whilst their rivals were to eventually commence operations and have, like Old Passage, become part of the national transport network.

Back in Bristol the *Princess* sported a new pale blue and yellow colour scheme but the *Queen* gathered moss, awaiting a buyer. Summer passed and both became part of the dockyard scene. In October the Highlands and Islands Development Board showed interest in the *Queen* and the Irish Company authorized Enoch Williams to negotiate on their behalf. Nothing came of this enquiry but after further consultation with Shannon Transport Systems Limited the *Severn Princess* and the *Severn Queen* were sold the following year to a new company associated with the Shannon backers called West of Ireland Fisheries Ltd. Hopes were raised that with the *Princess* on the Shannon the scheme could be got off the ground but after delivery to Foynes she remained laid up until removal under her own power to Limerick early in 1973 where she lay quietly rusting away.

On 29 January 1975 the Stephenson Clarke Shipping motor vessel *Angmering* had the misfortune to run aground loaded with 2,400 tons of coal on the Black Rock Shoal in Galway Bay. She was on a voyage from Gdansk in Poland to Galway but was stranded only three miles from her destination. She was declared a total loss and Oceanic Services Ltd. of Galway bought the cargo, the hull being purchased by Michael Bustard Shipping of Kent.

Salvage was the next problem. Oceanic Services proposed using an excavator aboard a barge but before anything was acquired they saw the *Severn Princess* advertised for sale. A visit was made to Limerick and inspection revealed her as perfectly suitable for their purposes. Successfully purchased she travelled the 110 nautical miles to Galway on 13 March 1975. A Lima dragline crane weighing twenty tons was placed on deck forward of the turn-table. Coal salvage began on April 15th with the *Severn Princess* moored to the port side of the *Angmering*, which was listing twenty-nine degrees to port. One very calm day 110 tons of coal were loaded leaving the aft decking three inches above the water level! Salvage of the coal was completed on 4 June, 1975.

Bustard's then hired the *Severn Princess* to carry salvage equipment in an attempt to refloat the wreck. Following a gale in late July the project was abandoned and the vessel broke in two on 2 January 1976 during a storm.

After the salvaging was finished the *Severn Princess* was used for bringing cargo to the three Aran Islands which are twenty-five to thirty miles west of Galway. Cargo brought to the Islands included 900 tons of coal, 400 tons of concrete blocks, 840 tons of top soil for an airstrip together with various items such as generators for an electrification scheme, cars, tractors, trucks, excavators, caravans, a prefabricated water reservoir et cetera. Currently she is being used to transport cargo to Aran and is to be hired for an engineering project in Killary Harbour.

The hull is now painted a bright red, and a new cabin with sleeping accommodation for four has been fitted on the port side beside the existing cabin and wheel-house. Decca Radar, V.H.F. and short wave radio transmitters and a large generator have also been installed.

It now seems that after languishing for almost ten years life has a new purpose for the *Severn Princess* in a manner that would probably surprise her original designers.

Her sister the *Severn Queen* was less fortunate. Beyond economical repair she was sold as she lay for £110 on 17 July 1969 to Cashmore's, scrap metal merchants at Newport. Two days later she crossed the Severn under her own power and was beached on the Usk, soon to become no more a happy memory under the breaker's hammer. Ben Brown managed to retrieve her builder's plate and telegraph for the sake of old times and the former now adorns his pub, the Five-Alls in Chepstow.

The *King* was to be reprieved for a little while longer but this is a story in itself.

CHAPTER SIXTEEN

A Demolition Job

Tuesday 25 October 1960 was a tragic day for shipping on the Severn Estuary. For years few serious accidents had occurred in these parts but severe river mist led to two tankers, waiting for the tide to rise to enter Sharpness Docks, drifting up river and colliding with each other and the Severn Railway Bridge between Lydney and Sharpness with disastrous results. Five men lost their lives in the fire that engulfed both vessels, the *Wastdale* and *Arkendale* of John Harkers. Severe damage was done to the bridge, two spans being torn adrift by the impact. This was a serious blow to British Railways who had been progressively strengthening the bridge for increased traffic. After much thought the bridge was written off and the problem of removal then arose; the idea of putting the bridge under 'care and maintenance' being dismissed as pointless.

A contract was taken out by British Rail with Nordman Construction Co. for the removal of the bridge. So as not to impede navigation simple demolition by explosives was ruled out and arrangements were made with Ulrich Harms of Hamburg for the hire of a floating crane capable of lifting down the heavy spans. The *Magnus II* had a lifting capacity of 400 tons but the two longest spans weighed 500 tons. They had to be literally pulled off the bridge but failed to fracture and fell complete into the river. Salvage proved difficult and much valuable metal sank beneath the shifting sand and mud of the river. The other spans were removed without incident to the river bank for breaking.

After the departure of *Magnus II* and the removal of the superstructure the problem of demolishing the remaining pillars arose. Henry Morgan of Nordman's wanted a broad vessel capable of carrying a crane on a stable platform but also able to sit on the river bed without fear of damage to the bottom or rolling over on the sloping river bank. At that time the Regent Oil Co. had several tankers laid up at Sharpness but these were really too narrow. A tanker of Harkers and a grain barge were also examined, the latter likely to have had a crane in the bow, but like the tanker she had insufficient beam.

It was mentioned that the Severn ferry-boats were laid up at Bristol and might be worth a look, so in the late autumn of 1967, a visit was made to the Albion Dockyard. The *King* was an obvious choice because she had an elevated bridge with unobstructed deck space beneath whereas the other two had island bridges.

With her broad 'flat' bottom and stable deck she was the most suitable vessel available in the area and negotiations were made with the Old Passage Ferry Co. for her purchase. She was bought as she lay for £3,250 and Nordman fitters were sent down to get her ready for sea.

Bill Hardy, a well-known salmon fisherman from Newnham, went down to skipper her but was alarmed at the state of the telegraph since there appeared to be no synchronization between the message indicated on the bridge and that shown in the engine-room. He departed and a chap called Ossie, an ex-merchant seaman took over with a crew of locals.

She had been insured through Lloyds for her purchase price from 3 April 1968 but if they had seen the pantomime enacted on the following 22nd May they might have had second thoughts. The crew cast off at the dockyard and the telegraph was given full ahead. Unfortunately the message received was the opposite to that intended and something akin to full astern was registered! She was eventually coaxed out of the Cumberland Basin and made an uneventful trip to Sharpness and then up the canal to Gloucester for fitting out. There the turn-table was removed and a Ruston caterpillar track crane, compressor and winch were installed. Both engines were overhauled but no structural alterations were made.

About two weeks later she returned to Sharpness and went into the Severn. She was insured solely for transporting metal from the dismantled bridge to Sharpness and a clause excluded any claims for damage caused by voluntary beaching; also owner's liability for any damage to third parties was fixed at £50,000.

Removal of the pillars proved difficult due to the soundness of their construction but waste material was normally dragged on to the boat and then dumped on a mud bank beneath the swing bridge over the canal. There another crane lifted the pieces on to lorries which utilized the bed of the railway as a road. When not in use the *King* was berthed in a natural channel close by which was a former course of the river. Difficulties were had with one engine but the prime problem was the lack of power in the strong currents which frequently reached eight or nine knots. Manning had its problems and one crew left after a strike and another lot were taken on. A new motor-boat was also smashed against the *King*'s hull whilst being pulled inboard. A hair-raising time was had by a few men on board one day when a mooring-rope parted and upon coming on deck they found themselves a mile up stream. Firm anchorages were a headache and slipped cables a constant hazard.

However hazards of another sort were in the offing. The contract was taking longer than expected and the original seven-month insurance had to be extended. Nordman's ran into financial difficulty and claims were made by creditors on the grounds of insolvency. Eventually the firm went into voluntary liquidation for reasons only partly connected with the Severn Bridge. Work continued at a reduced pace.

A rapid decision was then made by British Railways Western Region to take over the work themselves and work proceeded under the Gloucester District Civil Engineer, Mr J.E. Tyrer. A vast correspondence then poured forth arranging the transfer of stock and equipment and the letting of fresh contracts. It transpired that the *Severn King* was being purchased by a loan, the monthly repayments being taken over by the British Railways Board by arrangement with Nordman's Receiver Manager. Lloyds policy was transferred to the new operators from 1 February 1969, an extra premium being added for the carriage of explosives. Equipment handed over on that day consisted of the *King*, two Ruston cranes, a compressor and a winch. All were estimated by Nordman's Directors in the Receiver's Account as having a total realizable value of £7,200.

On 28 February 1969 British Rail officially took over the contract and work started again in earnest, scrap being off loaded from the *Severn King* to a stock-pile on top of the Southern Arm of the Old Entrance to Sharpness Dock.

The superintendent on site, Mr V.E. Harris, was the author of a weekly 'Progress Report' running for thirty-three weeks from week ending 8 February 1969 to week ending 20 September 1969, which is of great interest. Severe gales in the first week led to the captain and a labourer standing by on board the *King*. Considerable difficulties were had in May trying to secure the vessel in the area known as the whirlpool adjacent to No 19 and 20 pier stumps. The strength of the tide was underestimated and there were some unnerving moments when she was swept away until eventually brought under control and beached on the sand in the lee of the dock entrance. As a result of this mishap additional Sampson Posts were welded in to provide extra mooring points and a better anchor and additional chains purchased from Hill's at Bristol.

Equipment on the *King* consisted of the Ruston crane attached to the deck forward of the turn-table and an air compressor for use by Messrs Swinnerton & Miller, the explosives contractors. A great deal of time was taken in attempting to bore holes in the pillars to take the explosive charges. Having amassed sufficient scrap on the deck of the *King* she would then move to the southern arm to discharge. When not in use she would lie in the river near one of the piers. Bill Hardy of Newnham acted as ferryman for the crews when 'lying off' and was pilot and mooring supervisor for all movements in the channel.

Progress report No 22 was a momentous one for the *King*. Mr Harris reported "It was discovered on Saturday morning 5 July 1969 that the *Severn King* had moved forward on her moorings and sat on the remains of No 6 pier holing the ship and leaving her high and dry and listing badly, allowing the tides to wash over her stern and flood her engine-room. The stern mooring wire was still intact but the bow line had parted.

The size of the hole was two feet by five inches." Later Mr Tyrer sent a detailed report to Paddington in which he concluded that a strong south-westerly wind and the flood tide had exerted a heavy pull on the stern of the boat, causing the bow cable to 'snatch and part'. The *King* then swung on the stern cable across No 6 pier and settled on it as the tide receded. A piece of the pier casing pierced a hole approximately amidships.

At this time the *King* was being used mainly as a platform for the drilling compressor, her loss being a considerable inconvenience until some pontoons were eventually put into service.

Naturally enough the accident was front page news in the local press on the following Monday with pictures of a forlorn *King* perched precariously above the mud. Casting a critical eye over her condition Harker's agent noted that the deck had dropped, and thought that £10,000 was a rough estimate of the cost of the salvage and repair. This sum vastly exceeded her insured value and on 21 July 1969 a request to abandon was made to the Underwriters. Harker's salvaged her with the aid of a high tide several weeks later and brought her to the river bank. Harker's tender of £75 for the wreck was accepted and the vessel was then brought into Sharpness Harbour. Some difficulty was experienced in removing the engines as a hole had to be cut in the deck to remove the first one and the other slid across for removal via the same route. The plan was simple enough but the engine-room was so confined that it proved a tricky job. Stripped down the hull was then taken out on to the river bank up stream of the outer basin and beached at high water. Most of the structure was salvaged but today there are still the rusting bottom plates and stern hull structure protruding from the mud in a graveyard containing other interesting relics of the past.

Some doubt was expressed as to whom the proceeds of the insurance claim were to be credited but Nordman's receiver was of the opinion that, if the cost of completion (demolishing the bridge) exceeded Nordman's contract, then British Railways were entitled to recoup the excess from the proceeds of the sale of the *Severn King* and residual plant, estimated at £3,000.

Considering her long and faithful service it was an inglorious end to be sold for a paltry £75 but at least she was worth something to somebody.

The only other relic of this episode lies at Aust Pier itself. Gardiner of Brimscombe built a wooden motor barge in 1915 on the Stroud Canal for a local man. Named the *Halfren* she was Gloucester registered and transferred to the fleet of Benjamin Perry of Bristol in the 1920s but maintained her original port of registry. From that time until 1960 she operated between Avonside Wharf and Georges' Brewery in the City Docks, carrying barley and malt. Road freight took over from the rail/water combination in serving the enlarged brewery, now owned by Courages, and the long labouring little barge became surplus to requirements. In her youth she had been exchanged with a similar craft when Perry bought her, as her peg-leg owner found her difficult to manage. Now she was sold for fifty pounds to Upton Marine in November 1960 and used at Sharpness Railway Bridge for retrieving wreckage from the river bed. Unfortunately, lying aground probably strained her hull and the vessel was conveniently laid to rest at Aust where she is now rapidly falling apart.

It's regrettable that so few reminders of Stroudwater shipbuilding still exist.

Princess Ida *in close-up.*
Note turn-table with rope handles.

Rough crossing, pier hands stand in the swirling sea waiting for the
first rope at Aust March 1934.

Turn-table under construction aboard the Severn Queen *at the yard of Woodward & Scarr, Beverley, Yorks. 1934.*

Sideways launching — the Severn King *hits the water at Beverley, June 1935.*

Constructing the new Aust Pier, circa 1935.

Bank Holiday stranding at Beachley c.1938. Passage at low tide ceased hence the great pressure at peak periods to keep the customer happy at the risk of having to sit it out.

Pause for a smoke. Severn Queen *in war paint.
(L to R) James Hawker relief engineer, Charlie Savage skipper, Bo[...]
Jones engineer.
Courtesy Percy Palme[...]*

*A floating bridge? Construction under way at Newnham 1949 with
the prospect of a Severn crossing for heavy vehicles utilizing the
linked 'Lily-cans' in the foreground. The project failed due to
problems of stability.*

Recalcitrant Queen *returning under Chepstow Bridge with a sawn-off mast after breaking adrift 24th October 1953.*

Race Day. Punters arrive at Beachley aboard the Severn King *for Chepstow Races.* *Courtesy Daily Sketch*

Royal Patrons. Her Majesty Queen Elizabeth II and His Royal Highness The Duke of Edinburgh pass H.M.S. Venturer 24th April 1957 after their official tour of Worcestershire and Herefordshire.

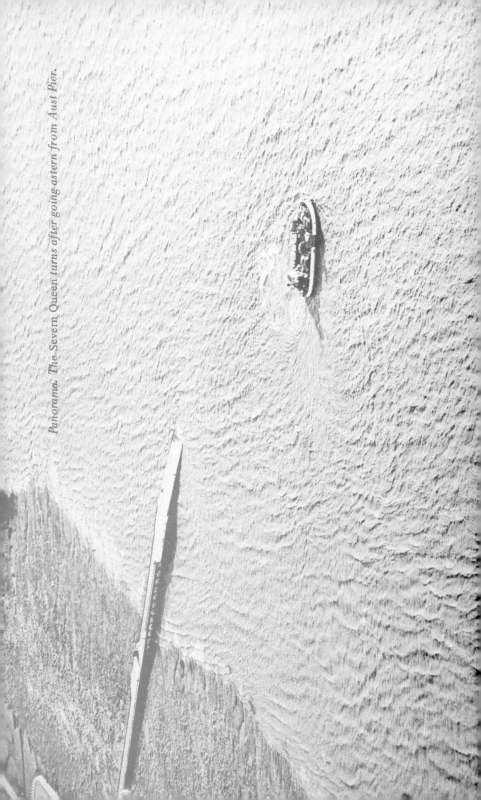

Panorama. The Severn Queen turns after going astern from Aust Pier.

New addition. **The Severn Princess** *leaves the ways of the Yorkshire Dry Dock Co. Ltd., 23rd May 1959.* *Courtesy Hull Daily Mail*

Frozen in 1962/63. Launch Mary B *and* Severn King. *Note twin funnels fitted to the King. This was the only occasion the service was suspended for any length of time.*

The Final Day. The Severn Princess dressed overall alongside Beachley Pier, opposite the Mary B.

Skipper Bill Groves.

Skipper Percy Palmer.

Lay up Albion Dockyard, Bristol December 1967. The three redundant ferry boats lie alongside the newly built Port of Bristol Dredger Clifton, minesweeper H.M.S. Venturer at Mardyke behind.
Courtesy Erik Hansen

Indomitable Welshman. Mr. Enoch Williams founder of The Old Passage Severn Ferry Co.

Construction 1870's style. Piles for The Severn Railway Bridge being sunk at Sharpness. The trow Victoria of Chepstow lies to the left.
Courtesy British Rail

Destruction 25th October 1960. Two tankers struck the bridge and exploded causing considerable damage. The Arkendale is depicted the day after with a length of railway track across her.

Courtesy British Rail.

Another victim. The Seven King noted on a partly demolished pund during demolition work July 1969.
Note the generator in the turn-table well and the Ruston crane for salvaging scrap.

Courtesy Dursley Gazette

salvage work. Here she is loading coal from the wrecked M.V. Angmering in Galway Bay.

Courtesy Oceanic Services Ltd

CHAPTER SEVENTEEN

Epilogue

Only ten years have passed since the bridge opened but it seems like an age. Beachley pier is as stout as ever but time and tide are taking their toll on the wooden timbers of Aust. Blackened beams lie at drunken angles ready to trap the unwary foot and send you spinning into the slime below. 1886 saw the ending of one era, 1966 another. Over a hundred years ago Thomas Fulljames, County Surveyor of Gloucestershire reported, "I am of the opinion that a bridge upon the suspension principle . . . is the most applicable on every account". I think he had Enoch's foresight but I wonder if it will be another Welshman who will ring the next change on the Severn Estuary. Many dream of a Severn Barrage uniting Welsh and English shores for ever. I wonder.

NOTES ON APPENDICES

Shares in any vessel are normally based on a division of the figure 64, thus sole ownership would be denoted as 64/64 and a part-share as 4/64 et cetera. Most vessels but not all are allotted an Official Number by the Registrar General of Shipping and Seamen. Where this was done the number is quoted. Measurements of a vessel were formerly taken in feet and inches but later it became the practice for figures to be quoted in feet and tenths of a foot, thus the *Severn King* was twenty-six feet and five tenths exact measurement overall breadth.

APPENDIX A

Vessels at Old Passage during the Nineteenth Century

1827-46 Old Passage Ferry Association, Beachley
Trustees: Chepstow Merchants Richard Jenkins, James Jenkins, Oliver Chapman and the Duke of Beaufort.
WORCESTER (*1*) Official No 10826 Wooden paddle steamer built by Wm. Scott & Son Bristol 1827 41 tons net, Length 65 feet 11 inches, Breadth 15 feet 4 inches, Depth 6 feet 3 inches, schooner rig two masts.
First crossing 13 June 1827, John Whitchurch master. Burnt to waterline 1837 and beached at Beachley. Remains rebuilt as schooner of 49 t.n., by Lydney shipbuilder Thomas Cheese Davies. Sold 1840 to Bridgwater interests as a collier. Further owners in Bristol Channel until sunk 7 December 1891 off Glamorgan Coast.

BEAUFORT Wooden paddle steamer built 1832 by Richard Watkins, Chepstow for a new consortium: Duke of Beaufort (26 shares) Arthur Wyatt, Monmouth (6) James Jenkins, Chepstow (13) George Rooke, Bigswear (19).
53 tons net, Length 70 feet 6 inches, Breadth 15 feet 5 inches, Depth 6 feet 5 inches; single cylinder engine.
Used by company elsewhere when ferry discontinued. Scrapped by 1860. Schooner rig two masts, one deck and a quarter deck.

WORCESTER (*2*) Official No 16346 Iron paddle steamer built 1838 by James & William Napier, Glasgow, entering service same year. Owners: Robert Castle Jenkins Esquire, Beachley (13) Duke of Beaufort (32) George Rooke Esquire, Bigswear (19).
60 tons gross, 17 net, Length 68 feet, Breadth 15 feet, Depth 7.5 feet. Two Masts, counter stern, woman's head figure-head. Designed to have a draught of 3 feet only. Broken up *circa* 1859.

1846-53 Bristol & South Wales Junction Railway.
No vessels. Right to operate purchased but not used.

APPENDIX B

Vessels at New Passage

1825-31 Charles Lewis, gentleman, of St Pierre and Thomas Walker, victualler, of Henbury, had 32 shares each in:
ST PIERRE Built 1825 by Pride & Williams, Newport, who also built engine. First steam vessel built at Newport. Wooden paddler 'sloop rig' single deck and cabin. Woman bust figure-head.
Length 55 feet 4 inches, Breadth 15 feet, Depth 6 feet 4 inches, 30 tons net.
Sold 1831 to J.T. Price, Neath Abbey. Converted to sail 1841. Sunk by 1855.

1846-53 Bristol & South Wales Junction Railway.
Right to operate purchased but no ferry operated.

1859-68 Bristol & South Wales Union Railway.
1868-86 Great Western Railway.
CYGNET A paddle steamer said to have been in Bristol and subsequently resold there. No other details known.

GEM Iron paddler built as the *LISCARD* in 1858 by James Napier at Govan for Wallasey Ferry on Mersey with engines by Forrester, Liverpool.
Length 122 feet, Breadth 18 feet, Depth 7.9 feet, 63 tons net, 100 gross.
Sold abroad 1861 but not delivered. Bought by E.R. Coulborn Renfrew. Registered Glasgow. Purchased June 1863 by B.S.W.U.R., with river cert. for 47 passengers. Sold 1864 for £1,050 by Mark Whitworth (Whitwell?) & Sons Bristol to Wallasey Board who had her rebuilt 1874 with Allsup engines. Wrecked 21 November 1881 *en route* to Brass River, W. Africa after sale to J. Lander, Birkenhead, on Porthlow Beach, Isles of Scilly.

RELIEF Official No 45374 Iron Paddle steamer built by M. Samuelson & Co., Hull 1862. Length 117.6 feet, Breadth 19.6 feet, Depth 10.1 feet, 93.82 tons net, 162.90 gross. Engines simple diagonal 2 cylinder 60 n.h.p. by Samuelsons. Built for

New Steam Tug Co., Liverpool. Purchased 11 September 1863 by B.S.W.U.R. but sold 1874 to Henry John Ward, Liverpool (St George's Steam Tug Co.) and renamed *MERSEY KING* Registered as tug/excursion vessel with river certificate for 563 passengers. Scrapped 1901.

PRESIDENT Wooden paddler built 1839 for Liverpool Steam Tug Co. by Thos. Raffield, N. Birkenhead. Length 114.4 feet, Breadth 21.4 feet, Depth 1.4 feet. Two cylinder engine. Net tonnage 113, gross 179. Held Mersey Passenger Certificate. 1859 sold Smith Stobart, collier proprietor, Penclawdd & William Bowen, shipbroker, Llanelly. Used R. Lougher coal-barge towage. April 1863 sold by James Habgood to B.S.W.U.R. Use uncertain. Sold 1865 to Oliver Morris, Bristol and broken up 1866 beneath Clifton Suspension Bridge.

DRAGON FLY Steam tender. In service 1863. No other details known.

CHRISTOPHER THOMAS Named after Chairman of B.S.W.U.R. Iron paddle steamer built for the company 1864 and delivered same year by Henderson, Coulborn & Co., Renfrew, who also built the 100 n.h.p. diagonal oscillating 4 cylinder engine. Length 132 feet, Breadth 20.2 feet, Depth 8.2 feet, 159 tons gross, 97 net. April 1890 sold to William S.Ogden, Cardiff, timber merchant and rebuilt at Chepstow with twin screws in 1891 coupled to two 2 cylinder Compound engines supplied by Plenty of Newbury. Revised weight 156 tons gross, 100 net.
February 1894 beached at Castlerock Strand, Coleraine, N. Ireland with extensive bottom damage. Salvaged and sold to African Association of Liverpool who sent her to Nigeria as a river trader. 1902 purchased to be sunk as a breakwater on Opobo River. Stranded *en route* and abandoned.

CHEPSTOW Iron paddler built 1874 by Hendersons with same engine as *Christopher Thomas*. Length 140.6 feet, Breadth 20.1 feet, Depth 8.2 feet. Sold to William Ogden and renamed *ROVER*. Rebuilt as per *Christopher Thomas* above. Revised weight 180 tons gross, 82 net. Sold to John Gunn, Cardiff 1895. Wrecked Nr. Youghal 7 July 1899.

APPENDIX C

Vessels at Old Passage Twentieth Century

1924-28 Consortia of Enoch Williams, Walter Watts and Samuel Dickinson Williams.

SILVER QUEEN Built by Boon Bros., Cleeves Yard, Northam, Nr. Appledore for Olney Bros. cost between £400 and £500 without engine to B.O.T. specification. Six cylinder Parsons petrol-paraffin marine engine of 50 h.p. at 800 r.p.m., fitted at Northam by Horace Olney. Length 48 feet Beam 13 feet Depth 5 feet 6 inches Draught 2 feet 6 inches to 3 feet for'ard. Black bottom white hull, varnished gun'ls and topsides. Black name. Derrick fitted for lifting motor cycles et cetera by Hurd Bros. & Henderson, Chepstow. Used as pleasure-boat at Barry until taken to Beachley to operate ferry to Aust 1926-28. Licensed to carry about 70. Returned to Barry to join Olney pleasure-fleet until sold *circa* 1939 to Lowestoft, travelling there via canals through Gloucester, taking three weeks. Subsequent fate unknown.

1931-1967 Old Passage Severn Ferry Co. Ltd.

MAY QUEEN Former Thames Police Launch purchased about 1918/19 by Monmouthshire Ship Co. Ltd., Chepstow (Now Fairfield-Maby) Rebuilt by them and used as a general workboat.

Sold 1931 to Old Passage for £100. Dimensions estimated as 26 feet x 8 feet with 18 inches draught. Power-International 30 h.p. 6 cylinder petrol/paraffin (tvo) mixture engine driving single screw. Capacity 30 passengers. Lost January 1936 in gale without trace after breaking moorings at Beachley.

PRINCESS IDA Built to order of Old Passage 1931 by Hurd Bros & Henderson, Chepstow. All wood single-screw passenger and vehicle ferry. Length 60 feet Breadth 20 feet Draught 1 foot 8 inches for'ard 3 feet aft Estimated speed 6 knots Power Elwe single cylinder diesel engine.

1941 Acquired by Royal Navy and attached to H.M.S. *Birnbeck*, Weston-super-Mare.

1945 Laid up at Castle Pill, Milford Haven. Eventually disintegrated.

SEVERN QUEEN Official No 162138 Built 1934 Woodward & Scarr, Beverley, Yorks. Steel twin screw motor passenger ferry. Registered Newport 5 January 1935 to Old Passage 64/64 shares. Length 75 feet Breadth 26.1 feet Depth of hold 6.5 feet Draught 4 feet 6½ inches aft 2 feet for'ard. Engine room length 16.1 feet.
Gross Tonnage 89.78 Registered Tonnage 45.85.
Twin two-stroke diesel engines by Crossley Bros Ltd. Manchester. Three 7 inch diameter cylinders 9 inch stroke. 150 b.h.p., 182 i.h.p. giving speed 8 knots.
Alterations to engines:
12 July 1950 four-stroke 6 cylinder Leyland diesels 4.8 inches diameter cylinders 5.5 inches stroke 22.14 n.h.p. 190 b.h.p. Speed 12 knots.
27 October 1950 Only details notified 34 n.h.p. 190 b.h.p. Speed 10 knots.
30 January 1959 four-stroke 6 cylinder Leyland diesels 5 inch diameter cylinders 5.75 inch stroke 7.5 n.h.p. 280 i.h.p. Speed 12 knots.
September 1966 laid up Chepstow, later at Cardiff. 10 November 1967 transferred to Albion Dockyard Bristol. 24 June 1969 sold to West of Ireland Fisheries Ltd., 14 Molesworth Street, Dublin. 19 July 1969 dep. 8.09 a.m. Cumberland Basin, Bristol to Cashmores Newport Sold £110 scrap broken up. Registry closed 5 January 1970.

SEVERN KING Official No 162139 Built 1935 Woodward & Scarr, Beverely, Yorks. Steel twin screw motor passenger ferry. Registered Newport 7 June 1935 to Old Passage 64/64 shares. Length 75.3 feet Breadth 26.1 feet Depth in hold 6.5 feet Draught 5 feet 6 inches aft 3 feet for'ard. Engine room length 16 feet Class 4 Passenger Certificate for 94 passengers. Gross Tonnage 83.09 Registered Tonnage 40.56. Twin two-stroke diesel engines by Crossley Bros. Ltd. Manchester. Three 5 inch diameter cylinders 9 inch stroke. 150 b.h.p., 184 i.h.p. giving speed 8 knots.
Alterations:
11 May 1951 four-stroke 5 cylinder Ruston & Hornsby of Lincoln diesels, 5 three-eight inch diameter cylinders. 8 inch stroke 6 n.h.p. 100 b.h.p. 118 i.h.p. Speed 10 knots.
1 January 1958 four-stroke 6 cylinder Leyland Ajax 0.680

diesels 5 inch diameter cylinders, 5.75 inches stroke. 15 n.h.p. 280 b.h.p. 350 i.h.p. Speed 10 knots.
1958 Twin funnels installed by Charles Hill, Albion Dockyard, Bristol September 1966 laid up at Chepstow, later at Cardiff. 10 November 1967 transferred to Albion Dockyard, Bristol. 8 May 1968 Sold to Nordman Construction Co. Ltd., North Dock, Commercial Road, Gloucester. Owner Henry E. Morgan, 1 Culross Close, Pittville, Cheltenham. Price £3,250. 22 May 1968 dep. 2.16 p.m. Bristol to Llanthony Wharf, Gloucester.
28 February 1969 taken over by British Rail. 5 July 1969 holed. 15 September 1969 wreck sold to Harker's Shipyard for £75. January 1970 broken up on foreshore Sharpness. 1976 bottom of hull still visible.

SEVERN PRINCESS Official No 183371 Built 1959 Yorkshire Dry Dock Co. Ltd., Hull. Steel twin screw motor car ferry Yard No 27. Registered Newport 9 November 1960 to Old Passage 64/64 shares. Length 77 feet Breadth 28 feet Depth in hold 6.6 feet Draught 4 feet six and a half inches aft two feet six inches for'ard. Engine room length 13.6 feet Class 4 Passenger Certificate for 94 Passengers. Gross Tonnage 96.47 Registered 56.21 Twin four-stroke 6 cylinder Leyland Ajax 0.680 diesels 5 inches diameter cylinders 5 three-quarter inch stroke 15 n.h.p. 290 b.h.p. 350 i.h.p. Speed 8 knots. Constructed to Lloyds A1 spec. 23 May 1959 launching.
September 1966 laid up at Chepstow, later at Cardiff. 10 November 1967 transferred to Albion Dockyard, Bristol. Overhauled February 1968 against pending sale to Shannon Transport Systems.
24 June 1969 Sold to West of Ireland Fisheries Ltd., 14 Molesworth Street, Dublin. Presumably operating company of S.T.S.
28 July 1969 Dep. 5.55 p.m. Bristol to Avonmouth prior to delivery to Foynes Ireland 2 August 1969, where laid up.
11 March 1970 West of Ireland Fisheries name changed to West of Ireland Ferries Ltd.
18 December 1973. Moved to Limerick Dock.
14 March 1975. Sold to Oceanic Services Ltd., 14 Cross Street, Galway.

13 March 1975. Dep.06.45 Limerick Dock Arr. Galway Harbour 19.00. Currently in service.

MARY B Thought to have been a former R.A.F. Seaplane Tender. Purchased as bare hull Leigh on Sea, Essex early sixties and overhauled by Chas Hill & Sons, Bristol. 44 feet long, 2 Ford Parsons of 150 n.h.p. installed. Hired to Associated Bridge Builders to 1966. Sold to Bombay, India thereafter.

All information on *Mary B* above hearsay.

APPENDIX D

Funnel Colours

Bristol & South Wales Union Railway

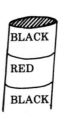

Old Passage Severn Ferry Co. Ltd

Houseflag — white with blue cross and red letters OPSF, one in each canton

APPENDIX E

Bibliography

The Somerset and Dorset Railway: R. Atthill. David & Charles, 1967

The Picture History of The Somerset and Dorset Railway: R. Atthill. David & Charles, 1970

Railway and other Steamers: Duckworth and Langmuir. Stephenson, 1968

West Country Passenger Steamers: G. Farr. Stephenson, 1967

Monmouthshire Sketchbook, No 637 to 639: F.J. Hando. South Wales Argus

Ferries and Ferrymen: G.B. Wood. Cassel, 1969

The Severn Tunnel its Construction and Difficulties 1872-1887: T.A. Walker. Kingsmead Press

Severn Bridge: L.T.C. Rolt

Wreck and Rescue in the Bristol Channel: G. Farr. Bradford Barton, 1966

The Secret War 1939/45: G. Pawle. Harrap, 1956

Railway Magazine, January 1970

British Railways Western Region Archives: District Civil Engineer, Gloucester

The Sphere: February 26th, 1949

Country Quest, Vol. 7 No. 4: September 1966

Mercantile Navy List Part 2, Motor Vessels: H.M.S.O.

Industrial Archaeology of the Bristol Region: A. Buchanan and N. Cossons. David & Charles, 1969

Industrial History in Pictures Bristol: A. Buchanan and N. Cossons. David & Charles, 1970

The Bristol Royal Mail: R.C. Tombs. J.W. Arrowsmith

The King's Post: R.C. Tombs. W.C. Hermans, 1905

Shipping Wonders of the World: C. Winchester. Fleetway House, London

Chepstow Ships: G. Farr. Chepstow Society, 1954

Directory of Stage Coach Services 1836: A. Bates. David & Charles, 1969

Westbury-on-Trym: E.H. Mogford, 1953

A Guide to Henbury: Hallen & Henbury Women's Institute, 1958

Annals of Bristol in the 18th Century: J. Latimer. Kingsmead Reprints, 1970

The Rise and Progress of Wallasey: E.C. Woods and P.C. Brown. Wallasey Corporation, 1960

The Death Ray Man The Biography of Grindell Matthews Inventor and Pioneer: E.H.G. Barwell. Hutchinson, 1946

Alway Family Papers

Newspapers in Avon County Archives, Bristol: *Bristol Evening Post, Bristol Evening World, Western Daily Press*. Articles in *Dursley Gazette, Gloucester Citizen, South Wales Argus, Western Mail and Echo, Hull Daily Mail, Illustrated London News*

Severn Bridge Tolls Act 1965 Section 11 and 12

The Severn & Wye Railway: H.W. Paar. David & Charles, 1963

APPENDIX F

Timetables

THE OLD PASSAGE SEVERN FERRY CO.
LTD.

Beachley-Aust Ferry

A Service Across the Severn

which effects a saving of 55 miles of roadway between South Wales and the West and South of England, for carrying Passengers, Cycles, Motor Cycles and Side Cars, will be

OPENED on
Monday, May 18, 1931

SUBJECT TO WEATHER, TIDE AND OTHER CIRCUMSTANCES, A PROMPT AND EFFICENT SERVICE WILL BE MAINTAINED.

BOAT LEAVES
BEACHLEY PIER ON THE HOUR
BOAT LEAVES
AUST PIER ON THE HALF HOUR

FARES—

ADULT PASSENGERS	1/-
JUVENILE PASSENGERS	6d.
BICYCLES	1/-
MOTOR CYCLES	1/6
MOTOR CYCLE and SIDE CAR	2/6

Motor Bus Services Both Sides of River

Fess Ltd., The Friary Cardiff

BEACHLEY-AUST FERRY

PASSENGER AND VEHICULAR TRANSPORT
BEACHLEY PIER

SEVERN KING

THE OLD PASSAGE SEVERN FERRY CO., LTD.

WINTER TIME TABLE AND INFORMATION

FEBRUARY 1966

A Half-Hourly Service will operate from Beachley and Aust Piers from:

(Broken lines denote breaks in service from low or high water)

	a.m.				p.m.
1 Tue.	9.00			until	4.30
2 Wed.	11.30	until 10.30 a.m.	1.00 p.m. until		4.30
3 Thu.	9.00		2.30 p.m. "		4.30
4 Fri.	9.00		3.30 p.m. "		4.30
5 Sat.	9.00				4.30
6 Sun.	9.00				1.00
7 Mon.	9.00				2.00
8 Tue.	9.00				3.00
9 Wed.	10.00				3.30
10 Thu.	10.30				4.00
11 Fri.	9.00 a.m.	9.30 a.m. until 11.30 a.m.		until	4.30
12 Sat.	9.00				4.30
13 Sun.	9.00				4.30
14 Mon.	9.00				4.30
15 Tue.	8.30				4.30
16 Wed.	9.00				4.30
17 Thu.	9.00		11.00 a.m. until		5.00
18 Fri.	9.00		12.30 p.m. "		5.00
19 Sat.	9.00		1.30 p.m. "		5.00
20 Sun.	8.30		3.00 p.m. "		5.00
21 Mon.	9.00		4.30 p.m. "		2.00
22 Tue.	9.00				2.30
23 Wed.	9.00				3.00
24 Thu.	9.00				3.30
25 Fri.	9.00				4.00
26 Sat.	9.00			until	4.30
27 Sun.	9.00				5.00
28 Mon.	8.30				5.00

MARCH 1966

A Half-Hourly Service will operate from Beachley and Aust Piers from:

(Broken lines denote breaks in service from low or high water)

	a.m.				p.m.
1 Tue.	9.00			until	5.30
2 Wed.	9.00				5.30
3 Thu.	9.00				5.30
4 Fri.	9.00	10.00 a.m.	12.30 p.m. until		5.30
5 Sat.	9.00	11.30 a.m.	2.00 p.m. "		5.30
6 Sun.	9.00	12.30 p.m.	3.00 p.m. "		5.30
7 Mon.	8.30	2.00 p.m.	5.00 p.m. "		2.30
8 Tue.	9.30				3.00
9 Wed.	10.00				3.30
10 Thu.	10.30				3.30
11 Fri.	9.00				4.00
12 Sat.	9.00				5.00
13 Sun.	8.30				5.30
14 Mon.	8.30				6.00
15 Tue.	9.00				6.00
16 Wed.	9.00				6.00
17 Thu.	9.00				6.00
18 Fri.	9.00	11.30 a.m.	1.00 p.m. until		6.00
19 Sat.	9.00	1.00 p.m.	4.00 p.m. "		7.00
20 Sun.	8.30	1.30 p.m.	4.00 p.m. "		7.00
21 Mon.	9.00	2.00 p.m.	4.30 p.m. "		7.00
22 Tue.	9.00	2.30 p.m.	5.00 p.m. "		7.00
23 Wed.	9.00	3.00 p.m.	5.30 p.m. "		7.00
24 Thu.	9.00	3.30 p.m.	6.00 p.m. "		7.00
25 Fri.	9.00	4.00 p.m.	6.30 p.m. "		7.00
26 Sat.	9.00	4.30 p.m.			7.00
27 Sun.	9.00				7.00
28 Mon.	8.30				7.00
29 Tue.	9.00			until	5.30
30 Wed.	9.00				7.00
31 Thu.	8.30				7.00

APRIL 1966

A Half-Hourly Service will operate from Beachley and Aust Piers from:

(Broken lines denote breaks in service from low or high water)

	a.m.				p.m.
1 Fri.	9.00			until	7.00
2 Sat.	9.00	11.00 a.m.	1.30 p.m. until		7.30
3 Sun.	9.00	12.00 noon	3.00 p.m. "		7.30
4 Mon.	8.30	1.00 p.m.	5.00 p.m. "		7.30
5 Tue.	9.00	1.30 p.m.	5.30 p.m. "		7.30
6 Wed.	9.30	2.30 p.m.	6.00 p.m. "		7.30
7 Thu.	10.00	3.00 p.m.	6.30 p.m. "		7.30
8 Fri.	10.30	3.30 p.m.	7.00 p.m. "		7.30
9 Sat.	9.00	4.00 p.m.			4.30
10 Sun.	9.00				5.00
11 Mon.	8.30				6.00
12 Tue.	9.00				6.30
13 Wed.	9.00				7.30
14 Thu.	9.00				7.30
15 Fri.	9.00			until	7.30
16 Sat.	9.00				7.30
17 Sun.	8.30	11.30 a.m.	1.30 p.m. until		7.30
18 Mon.	8.30	12.30 p.m.	2.30 p.m. "		7.30
19 Tue.	9.00	1.00 p.m.	3.30 p.m. "		7.30
20 Wed.	9.00	1.30 p.m.	4.00 p.m. "		7.30
21 Thu.	9.00	2.00 p.m.	5.30 p.m. "		7.30
22 Fri.	9.00	2.30 p.m.	6.00 p.m. "		7.30
23 Sat.	9.00	3.00 p.m.	6.30 p.m. "		7.30
24 Sun.	8.30	3.30 p.m.	7.00 p.m. "		7.30
25 Mon.	8.30	4.30 p.m.			7.30
26 Tue.	9.00	5.00 p.m.		until	5.30
27 Wed.	9.00				7.00
28 Thu.	9.00				7.30
29 Fri.	9.00				7.30
30 Sat.	9.00				7.30

FARES

		SINGLE		SINGLE
Passengers		1/-	Motor Cars (with Drivers)	8/6, 9/6,
Juvenile Passengers		6d.	10/6 and 12/6 (according to length)	
Bicycle (and Rider)		2/-	Lorries, Vans, Shooting Brakes	8/6 to 25/-
Motor Cycle (and Rider)		3/-	(according to size of vehicle)	
Motor Cycle Combination (with Driver)		5/-	Advance Bookings cannot be made	

Conditions of carriage appear on Tickets and are displayed in the Company's Offices.

OFFICIAL TIME TABLE

Phones: Beachley, Pier 2212 Chepstow

Aust Pier - 219 Pilning

Residence - 2068 Chepstow

THE OLD PASSAGE SEVERN FERRY Co., Ltd.

BEACHLEY PIER, Near CHEPSTOW,

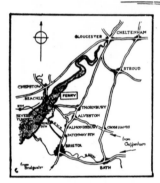

BEACHLEY ~ AUST FERRY.

A Service across the Severn at the point indicated on the map shewn, by Swift Motor Craft, carrying Motor Cars, Passengers, Cycles, Motor Cycles and Side-Cars, Light Delivery Vans and 30 cwt. Lorries.

Motor Cars and Passengers, Motor Cycles, and Side-Cars, by using the Ferry the road distance saved between Bristol and South Wales is **55** Miles.

TIME TABLE

WEEKDAYS & SUNDAYS for MARCH, 1933.

Weather, tide and circumstances permitting.

LEAVE BEACHLEY.									MARCH			LEAVE AUST.								
A.M. times light figures.				P.M. times dark figures.								A.M. times light figures.				P.M. times dark figures.				
		10*30	11*30	12 30	1 30	2 30	3 30		1	Wednesday	1		11*0	12 0	1 0	2 0	3 0			
		10*30	11*30	12 30	1 30	2 30	3 30	4 30	2	Thursday	2		11*0	12*0	1 0	2 0	3 0	4 0		
		10*30	11*30	12 30	1 30	2 30	3 30	4 30	3	Friday	3		11*0	12 0	1 0	2 0	3 0	4 0	5 0	
	9 30	10 30	11 30	12 30	1 30	2 30	3 30	4 30 5 30	4	Saturday	4	10 0	11*0	12 0	1 0	2 0	3 0	4 0	5 0	
	9 30	10 30	11 30	12 30	1 30	2 30	3 30	4 30 5 30	5	Sunday	5	10 0	11 0	12 0	1 0	2 0	3 0	4 0	5 0	
8 30	9 30	10 30	11 30	12 30	1 30	2 30	3 30	4 30 5 30	6	Monday	6	9 0 10 0	11 0	12 0	1 0	2 0	3 0	4 0	5 0	
	9 30	10 30	11 30	12 30	1 30	2 30	3 30	4 30 5 30	7	Tuesday	7	10 0	11 0	12 0	1 0	2 0	3 0	4 0	5 0	
	9 30	10 30	11 30	12 30	1 30	2 30	3 30	5 30	8	Wednesday	8	10 0	11 0	12 0	1 0	2 0	3 0	4 0		
	9 30	10 30		12 30	1 30	2 30	3 30	4 15	9	Thursday	9	10 0	11 0		1 0	2 0	3 0			
	9 30	10 30	11 30			2 30	3 30	4 30	10	Friday	10	10 0	11 0				3 0	4 0	5 0	
	9 30	10 30	11 30	12 30			3 30	4 30 5 15	11	Saturday	11	10 0	11 0	12 0				4 0	5 0	
	9 30	10 30	11 30	12 30	1 30			4 30 5 30	12	Sunday	12	10 0	11 0	12 0	1 0			4 0	5 0	
		10 30	11 30	12 30	1 30			4 30 5 30 6 15	13	Monday	13		11 0	12 0	1 0	2 0			5 0	
		10 30	11 30	12 30	1 30			5 30 6 30	14	Tuesday	14		11 0	12 0	1 0	2 0				
	9 15		11 30	12 30	1 30	2 30		6 30	15	Wednesday	15	9 45		12 0	1 0	2 0	3 0			
		10*30	11 30	12 30	1 30	2 30	3 30	6 30	16	Thursday	16		11*0	12 0	1 0	2 0	3 0			
		10*30	11*30	12 30	1 30	2 30	3 30	6 30	17	Friday	17		11*0	12*0	1 0	2 0	3 0	4 0		
		10*30	11*30	12 30	1 30	2 30	3 30	4 30	18	Saturday	18		11*0	12*0	1 0	2 0	3 0	4 0	5 0	
	9 30	10 30	11*30	12 30	1 30	2 30	3 30	4 30 5 30	19	Sunday	19	10 0	11 0	12*0	1 0	2 0	3 0	4 0	5 0	
8 30	9 30	10 30	11 30	12 30	1 30	2 30	3 30	4 30 5 30 6 30	20	Monday	20	9 0 10 0	11 0	12 0	1 0	2 0	3 0	4 0	5 0	
	9 30	10 30	11 30	12 30	1 30	2 30	3 30	4 30 5 30 6 30	21	Tuesday	21	10 0	11 0	12 0	1 0	2 0	3 0	4 0		
	9 30	10 30	11 30	12 30	1 30	2 30	3 15		22	Wednesday	22	10 0	11 0	12 0	1 0	2 0	3 0	4 45		
	9 30	10 30	11 30		1 30	2 30	3 30		23	Thursday	23	10 0	11 0		1 0	2 0	3 0	4 0		
	9 30	10 30	11 30			2 30	3 30	4 30	24	Friday	24	10 0	11 0				3 0	4 0	5 0	
	9 30	10 30	11 30	12 30			3 30	4 30	25	Saturday	25	10 0	11 0	12 0	1245			4 0	5 0	
	9 30	10 30	11 30	12 30	1 30			4 30 5 30	26	Sunday	26	10 0	11 0	12 0	1 0				5 0	
		10 30	11 30	12 30	1 30			4 30 5 30	27	Monday	27		11 0	12 0	1 0	2 0			5 0	
8 30		10 30	11 30	12 30	1 30	2 30		5 30 6 30	28	Tuesday	28	9 0	11 0	12 0	1 0	2 0				
		10*30	11 30	12 30	1 30	2 30	3 30	5 30 6 30	29	Wednesday	29		11*0	12 0	1 0	2 0	3 0			
		10*30	11 30	12 30	1 30	2 30	3 30	5 30 6 30	30	Thursday	30		11*0	12 0	1 0	2 0	3 0			
		10*30	11 30	12 30	1 30	2 30	3 30	5 30 6 30	31	Friday	31		11*0	12 0	1 0	2 0	3 0	4 0		

* Denotes when Motor Cars cannot be carried, only Motor Cycles and Side-Cars.

There is a convenient Motor Bus Service between Chepstow and Beachley, and between Bristol and Aust. both services run right to the Ferry piers.

FARES.

			SINGLE			
Adult Passengers	....	....	1/-	Motor Cycle and Side-Car	....	
Juvenile Passengers	....	....	6d.	Motor Cars under 8 H.P. (with Driver)		
				Book of Six 5/- Tickets, £1/4/-		
Bicycles	....	....	1/-	Motor Cars over 8 H.P.	,,	,,
Motor Cycles	....	....	1/6	Book of Six 6/- Tickets, £1/10/-		

SPECIAL DAY RETURN PASSENGER FARE, 1/-

APPENDIX G

Traffic Figures

Old Passage Severn Ferry Co. Ltd.
Accurate statistical analysis is difficult due to gaps in company records but all the figures available are detailed below.

PERIOD	PASSENGERS	CARS	LORRIES	MOTOR/PEDAL CYCLES
1931/32	26,000	6,000	N/A	N/A
April - June 1933	8,435	3,222		N/A
January - June 1934	9,458	5,212		N/A
1935	114,650	43,218	556	10,924

Figures produced for Severn Bridge Inquiry:
1931-35 Passengers 256,771; Pedal-cycles 17,624; Motor cycles 14,903; Combinations 3,015; Lorries 846; Cars under 8 h.p., 18,959, over 8 h.p., 65,823.

PERIOD	PASSENGERS	VEHICLES
3rd Jan - 20th March 1936	4,251	2,588
27th March - 8th May 1936	10,085	7,301
15th May - 3rd July 1936	18,540	14,190
7th Aug - 4th Sept 1936	27,599	13,499
11th Sept - 31st Dec 1936	18,537	19,371
8th Jan - 2nd April 1937	13,602	13,600
2nd July - 1st Oct 1937	64,368	40,158
1st April - 13th May 1938	16,686	14,981
20th May - 1st July 1938	22,279	17,964
8th July - 30th Sept 1938	67,143	42,305
7th Oct - ? Dec 1938	14,640	15,823
6th Jan - 9th June 1939	40,243	42,984
5th Jan - 29th March 1940	14,778	11,842
12th July - 27th Sept 1940	49,919	14,844
11th Jan - 27th Dec 1940	10,264*	12,191
4th July - 23rd Sept 1941	39,300	24,004
3rd Oct - 26th Dec 1941	13,586	12,978
2nd Jan - 27th March 1942	8,943	11,703
3rd April - 2nd Oct 1942	41,559	23,861
8th Jan - 26th Mar 1943	3,170	10,288
9th July - 31st Dec 1943	17,654	10,649
7th Jan - 30th June 1944	16,972	12,367
7th July - 30th Sept 1944	20,982	6,666
6th Oct - 22nd Dec 1944	4,517	5,680
1st Jan - 31st March 1945	12,393	5,576
6th April - 29th June 1945	18,082	10,146

6th July - 5th Oct 1945	44,223	21,351
12th Oct - 31st Dec 1945	9,518	8,474
1946	96,079	74,973
1st Jan - 30th June 1947	37,978	31,554
Estimate July/August	8,500	15,000
1st Sept - 31 Dec 1947	17,559	19,420
1948	98,401	73,275
1949	127,278	82,274
1950	135,783	91,329
1951	166,649	110,831
1952	174,365	120,054
1953	177,994	113,097
1954	188,777	130,983
1955	187,066	142,558
1956	200,224	134,199
1957	185,315	136,758
1958	200,269	145,752
1959	244,511	170,872
6th April - 28th Dec 1960	260,403**	162,567(172,000)
1961	279,940	199,947
1st Jan 1962 - 2nd Jan 1963	436,998	185,105
3rd Jan 1963 - 1st Jan 1964	426,402	182,776
2nd Jan - 31st Dec 1964	472,543	209,182
1965	287,144	204,286
1st Jan - 8th Sept 1966	197,739	165,144

*some weeks missing
**275,000 est. 1960

The growth of traffic in post-war years was phenomenal as illustrated by these figures but this only increased the problems of seasonal demand illustrated on a lesser scale by the pre-war figures. The opening of the Severn Bridge has removed most of the headaches of peak demand but the exposed site still means restrictions due to bad weather from time to time.